Vocabulary Workout for the SSAT/ISEE

Volume 2

JJMG Enterprises LLC
30 N. Gould St.
Suite N
Sheridan, WY 82801
USA

Editorial:
Justin Grosslight, head author and editor.

First Edition, 2017

ISBN: 978-0-9984841-7-4

10 9 8 7 6 5 4 3 2 1

Vocabulary Workout for the SSAT/ISEE

Volume 2

Justin Grosslight

Published by JJMG Enterprises LLC

Preface

Becoming an expert in any language is hard work. Regardless of whether English is your mother tongue, more advanced reading and vocabulary skills often accrue slowly and only with a sustained commitment to reading intricate material. Because of this, transitioning from communicating in popular English to becoming a consumer of scholarly and intellectual prose can be arduous work. While there is no supplement for reading erudite materials, building a vocabulary and an understanding of intellectual concepts is critical for language mastery.

In writing this edition of *Vocabulary Workout*, I had in mind the myriad individuals who are fluent in conversational English but who want to take their writing and vocabulary skills to the next level, especially those prepping for their SSAT and ISEE exams. Many of today's students and professionals seek to develop these skills, but find the task extraneous to their immediate needs, overly pedantic, or simply time consuming. *Vocabulary Workout* is meant to ease that process. Unlike other vocabulary books, many of which are merely extended word lists, this book is replete with exercises; there are also lessons to help you understand roots of words and intellectual terms. And the words are useful: they have been gleaned from statistical examination of SSAT and ISEE college exams, which, in turn, excerpt their readings from a wide array of sophisticated prose materials.

These words are suitable for either classroom study or independent preparation. Do note, however, that the words in this book do not constitute an exhaustive vocabulary list necessary for success. This book is the second of two volumes used to help students prepare for their SSAT and ISEE exams. One can also purchase a complete edition of *Vocabulary Workout* that combines the contents of both volumes into one text.

Writing this book has been an evolving process, and I have enjoyed receiving feedback as it develops. In particular, I would like to thank Robert Fouldes, Nicoleta Marinescu, Tracy Nguyen, and Sonya Petkova for their contributions, sustained support, proofreading, and constructive criticism. Several students – Jack Le, Tram Huynh, Thanh Doan, Quoc Huynh, Tan Khoa, Trong Phan – have gladly provided input, corrected errors, and given frank suggestions as they used drafts of this book to prepare for their SSAT examinations. Marion Vangaeveren has done a fabulous job with the book's cover artwork.

I hope that this book will be as immensely useful to you as it has been for the students who used it in its gestation period. With that said, good luck on your vocabulary endeavors!

Justin Grosslight

How to Use This Book

This book is intended to help build your vocabulary; it is a strategically organized catalogue of words that appear in intellectual and scholarly English, especially on secondary school entrance examinations. It is not, however, intended to be your sole source of learning words. Ideally, this book should be used in tandem with reading other scholarly and intellectual materials to help nurture your vocabulary growth.

Often to fully understand a word and its meaning(s), it is helpful to see a word in context many times. To reinforce this idea, the exercises contained in this book often require dictionary use. By looking up words in a dictionary, you can read samples of their uses in various settings and then apply what you have learned to the exercises in this text. Doing so will provide an active approach to building a vocabulary. This book's exercises also use a consistent intellectual vocabulary to complement the focal words of each lesson. Learning these words should further enhance your verbal skills.

At a stable pace, one should be able to absorb approximately fifty words, or ten lessons, per week. We have provided review quizzes after every ten lessons to help facilitate your study. One can study more words, of course, but diminishing returns may occur if more than twenty lessons are absorbed each week. Ideally this book should be studied at a moderate pace consistently over a long duration, allowing for time to let words sink in slowly. There are also many reasons why someone should use this book: whether you want to build a more solid vocabulary, you want to prepare for an examination, or you simply hope to sound erudite, all are good reasons for using this text. Whatever your purpose of study, however, it is imperative that you not give up on learning words.

Possessing a solid vocabulary can help you get in a good academic program, can make you more attractive for a corporate job, and can make you sound more articulate and knowledgeable. We hope you enjoy your endeavor to broaden your vocabulary with *Vocabulary Workout*!

TABLE OF CONTENTS

The Origins of English

English belongs to the family of Indo-European languages, which today comprise many languages spoken on the Earth. Most directly, the roots of English lay with Latin, the language of the Roman Empire that was spoken in the Mediterranean region two thousand years ago. From Latin emerged two families of European languages, Romance Languages and Germanic Languages. English is a Germanic language by structure and heritage, but also has borrowed much in style and vocabulary from French over the centuries (hence its proximity to French on the chart below). Many of the origins of English words stem from Latin, and still more come from Greek. The dashed line connecting Greek and Latin indicates that the languages had a cultural overlap, but that the former did not directly spawn the latter.

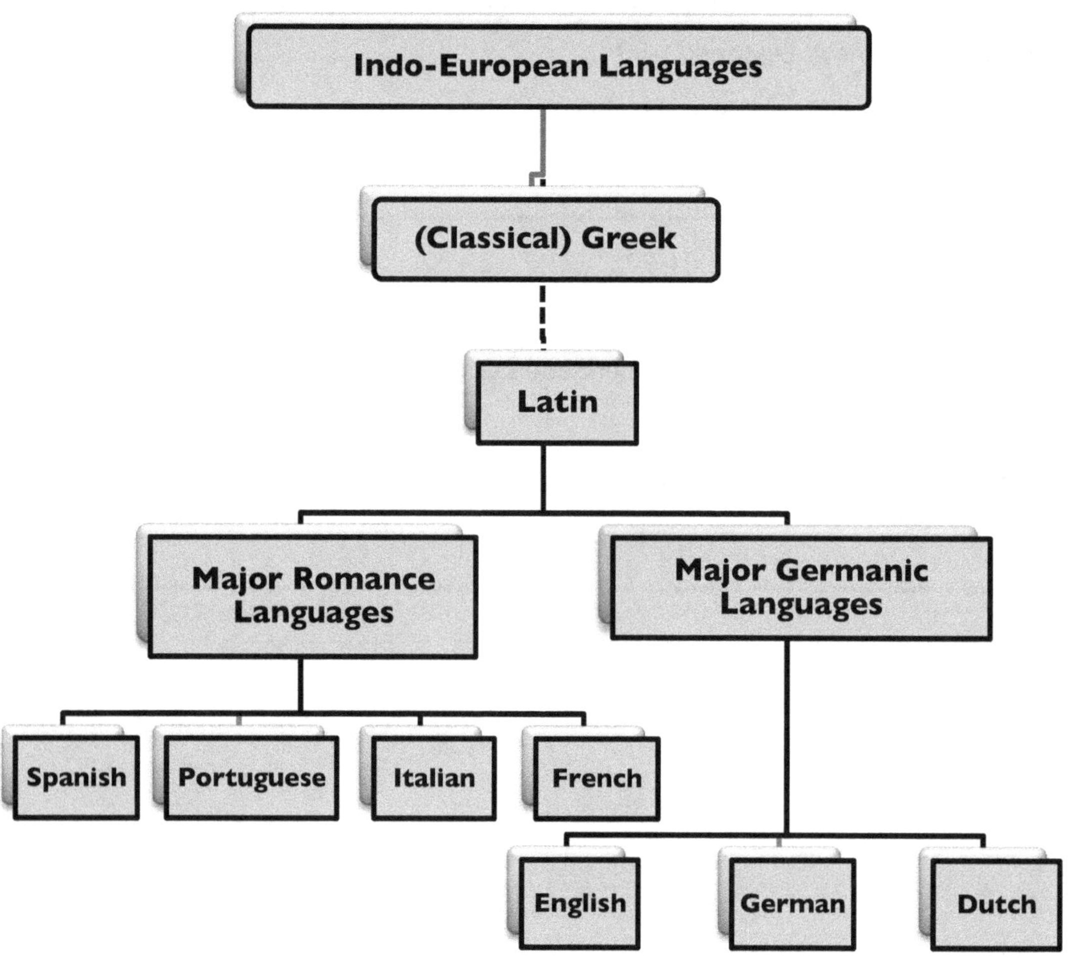

Lesson 1

THE DILIGENT ART STUDENT

Maria prided herself on being an **intellectual** who could **embrace** new and diverse opinions on art. Moreover, she was **diligent** in her studies of new artistic trends. Whenever she had an essay to write, she did not like to **generalize**; on the contrary, she would research many specific details about the issue in question. She knew that artistic tastes were quite **fickle** and could change very quickly. Thus, Maria strove to keep herself updated on artistic topics so that she could be an effective critic.

NEW WORDS

intellectual
ˌintlˈekCHo͞oəl

embrace
emˈbrās

generalize
ˈjenərəˌlīz

fickle
ˈfikəl

diligent
ˈdiləjənt

Definitions: Try matching the words in the list with the appropriate definitions. If you are stuck, check the glossary in the back of the book or the passage at the top of the page.

1.	intellectual ________	a.	changing one's loyalties, interests, or affection frequently
2.	embrace ________	b.	(n.) the act of holding someone closely in one's arms; (v.) 1. to hold someone closely in one's arms; 2. to accept or support a belief, theory, or change willingly and enthusiastically; 3. to include or contain something as a constituent part
3.	generalize ________	c.	to make a general or broad statement by inferring from specific cases; to make something more widespread or common
4.	fickle ________	d.	(adj.) of or relating to use of mental faculties; possessing highly developed mental faculties; (n.) a person with highly developed mental faculties
5.	diligent ________	e.	having or showing care and conscientiousness in one's work or duties

Sentences: Try to use the words above in a sentence below. Remember that a word ending may be changed or its figure of speech slightly altered.

6. Universities are excellent places to have myriad ________________ discussions.
7. Dale is ________________ and changes her mind about nearly everything.
8. Seeing the twins ________________ each other after a long separation was moving.
9. It is hard to ________________ whether a student will be successful in my history course based on one five-minute quiz.
10. As a(n) ________________ realtor, Annette previews the properties that she sells.

Lesson 2

NEW WORDS

wax
waks

noisome
ˈnoisəm

beneficial
ˌbenəˈfiSHəl

optimal
ˈäptəməl

encumber
enˈkəmbər

DISCORD AT THE FASHION COMPANY

The conflict between the two designers would **wax** very quickly and they often threw **noisome** and hurtful remarks at each other. This constant discord was not **beneficial** for anyone at the office. Because the two did not work together well, the company could not operate at an **optimal** level. The arguments between the two main designers would greatly **encumber** the creative process and the company's popularity slowly waned.

Definitions: Try matching the words in the list with the appropriate definitions. If you are stuck, check the glossary in the back of the book or the passage at the top of the page.

1.	wax	________	a.	to restrict or burden someone or something in such a way that free action or movement is difficult; to saddle a person with debt or mortgage; to fill or block up (a place)
2.	noisome	________	b.	favorable or advantageous; resulting in good
3.	beneficial	________	c.	best or most favorable
4.	optimal	________	d.	to become larger or stronger
5.	encumber	________	e.	having an extremely offensive smell; disagreeable; unpleasant

Sentences: Try to use the words above in a sentence below. Remember that a word ending may be changed or its figure of speech slightly altered.

6. Research shows that, in general, the ________________ amount of sleep time for humans is eight hours.
7. Philippa's interest in the mayoral race ________________ as she heard that her best friend would be seeking office.
8. When a skunk feels threatened, it emits a ________________ scent.
9. It is ________________ to eat healthfully and to exercise daily.
10. It is important not to let your workload ________________ you.

Lesson 3

A GOOD MATCH

David possesses an almost **celestial** beauty – a **ruddy** tan that accentuates his lean and strong muscles, beautiful blonde locks that are carelessly brushed back, and piercing blue eyes that soften every time he smiles. Add to the mix his cheerful **disposition** and a wisdom that tends to **accrue** with each passing day. With such traits, David can easily **enthrall** most women that he meets. His girlfriend Jane often wonders why he fell in love with her, without realizing that her unique charm, intelligence, and sense of humor are just as attractive as David's.

> **NEW WORDS**
>
> **celestial**
> səˈlesCHəl
>
> **ruddy**
> ˈrədē
>
> **enthrall**
> enˈTHrôl
>
> **accrue**
> əˈkro͞o
>
> **disposition**
> ˌdispəˈziSHən

Definitions: Try matching the words in the list with the appropriate definitions. If you are stuck, check the glossary in the back of the book or the passage at the top of the page.

1.	celestial	________	a.	1. a person's inherent qualities of mind and character; 2. the way in which something is placed or arranged, especially in relation to other things
2.	ruddy	________	b.	(adj.) having a healthy red or reddish color; (v.) to make reddish in color
3.	enthrall	________	c.	to capture the fascinated attention of
4.	accrue	________	d.	(of sums of money or benefits) to be received by someone in regular or increasing amounts over time
5.	disposition	________	e.	of or pertaining to the sky or the heavens

Sentences: Try to use the words above in a sentence below. Remember that a word ending may be changed or its figure of speech slightly altered.

6. Interest will ____________________ in most savings accounts if left untouched over time.
7. Laney was ____________________ with the idea of being promoted to a chair on the board of directors for her company.
8. Mars is called "the red planet" because of its ____________________ appearance.
9. Part of the reason that Shikha is so likeable is because of her warm and pleasant ____________________.
10. Though astronomy and astrology both concern ____________________ matters, the former is a science while the latter is used to assess the influence of heavenly bodies on human affairs.

NEW WORDS

manipulate
məˈnipyəˌlāt

linchpin
ˈlinCHˌpin

erroneous
iˈrōnēəs

enlighten
enˈlītn

hasten
ˈhāsən

Lesson 4

MAINTAINING THE PARTY'S REPUTATION

The famous politician was the **linchpin** of the newly found party. Thus when he got involved in a scandal, other political parties tried to **manipulate** the situation and discredit the whole organization. To think that the party would completely fall apart was an **erroneous** assumption, however. The new party's spokespeople did indeed **hasten** to refute the accusations. They did their best to **enlighten** the public about important details regarding the scandal that dissociated the party itself from the politician's actions.

Definitions: Try matching the words in the list with the appropriate definitions. If you are stuck, check the glossary in the back of the book or the passage at the top of the page.

1. manipulate ________
2. linchpin ________
3. erroneous ________
4. enlighten ________
5. hasten ________

a. a person or thing vital to an enterprise or organization
b. to give (someone or several people) greater knowledge and understanding about a subject or situation
c. to be quick to do something; to move hurriedly
d. wrong, incorrect
e. 1. to handle or control (a tool, mechanism, etc.) in a skillful manner; to edit, alter, or move text or data on a computer; 2. to control or influence a person or situation cleverly, unscrupulously, or unfairly; to alter data or present statistics so as to mislead

Sentences: Try to use the words above in a sentence below. Remember that a word ending may be changed or its figure of speech slightly altered.

6. In an effort to ____________________ the progress of building the skyscraper, workers were given increased hours and salaries.
7. The cunning politician tried to ____________________ other people into voting for him by making false promises in his campaign speeches.
8. Margot is the ____________________ that holds this academic program together; if she retires, its fate will be put into question.
9. The purpose of the conference is to ____________________ people about the importance of receiving a university education.
10. Marlene had to defend herself against ____________________ claims that she had stolen her sister's wallet and money.

Lesson 5

THE DOWN-TO-EARTH ARTIST

The young dancer often received ample **praise** for her **lithe** body and graceful movements. However, she did not let those flatteries go to her head. She continued to focus on her work and improvement. She knew that praise and fame were a part of the show business **gloss**. She was also aware that in the world of show business sincerity was **scarce**. Therefore, she was not surprised when criticisms came; in fact, she was able to **weather** all such negative remarks with the same calm and determined attitude with which she received all positive feedback.

NEW WORDS

lithe
līTH̲

praise
prāz

weather
ˈweTH̲ər

gloss
gläs, glôs

scarce
ske(ə)rs

Definitions: Try matching the words in the list with the appropriate definitions. If you are stuck, check the glossary in the back of the book or the passage at the top of the page.

1.	lithe	__________	a.	(of food, money, or another resource) insufficient for the demand; occurring in small numbers or quantities
2.	praise	__________	b.	(n.) a shine or luster on a smooth surface; (v.) to conceal or disguise something by treating it briefly or representing it misleadingly
3.	weather	__________	c.	(n.) the state of the atmosphere at a place and time as regards heat, precipitation, humidity, etc.; (v.) 1. to wear away and change the texture of something by long exposure to the atmosphere; 2. to come safely through a storm or turbulent situation
4.	gloss	__________	d.	(especially of a person's body) thin, supple, graceful
5.	scarce	__________	e.	(n.) the expression of approval or admiration of someone or something; (v.) to express warm approval of

Sentences: Try to use the words above in a sentence below. Remember that a word ending may be changed or its figure of speech slightly altered.

6. Funke was disappointed when her professor ____________________ over her paper instead of giving it a thorough read.
7. The ____________________ in equatorial regions is warmer than it is in arctic regions.
8. People with ____________________ bodies are able to stretch well in exercises.
9. Though not impossible to find, albino individuals are truly ____________________.
10. Receiving ____________________ from Joan is a big deal, as she rarely ever gives anyone or anything a compliment.

Lesson 6

NEW WORDS

warp
wôrp

resuscitate
riˈsəsəˌtāt

endeavor
enˈdevər

mendicant
ˈmendikənt

ferocious
fəˈrōSHəs

LAWS OF THE URBAN JUNGLE

A policeman was trying to **resuscitate** a **mendicant** who had fallen unconscious on the street. The officer made many an **endeavor** to revive him, but to no avail. Though this policeman's determination to save the man was **ferocious**, it seemed that the homeless guy was too weak to overcome the hunger and dehydration sapping his vitality. Though bystanders were bewildered by the officer's ardor, optimism was the cornerstone of the policeman's personal philosophy. For him, neither stereotypes nor negative prior experiences with homeless people could **warp** his vision that all humans are created equal and deserve a fair shot at life.

Definitions: Try matching the words in the list with the appropriate definitions. If you are stuck, check the glossary in the back of the book or the passage at the top of the page.

1. warp __________ a. savagely fierce, cruel, or violent
2. resuscitate __________ b. (adj.) given to begging; (n.) a beggar
3. endeavor __________ c. to revive someone from unconsciousness or apparent death; to make an idea or enterprise vigorous again
4. mendicant __________ d. (n.) an attempt to achieve a goal; an enterprise or undertaking; (v.) to try hard to do or achieve something
5. ferocious __________ e. to bend or cause to become bent out of shape, typically because of dampness

Sentences: Try to use the words above in a sentence below. Remember that a word ending may be changed or its figure of speech slightly altered.

6. The ____________________ approached me on the sidewalk and asked if I could donate a dollar to him.
7. If someone has a heart attack, the goal of emergency medical services is to ____________________ that person.
8. Most people view tigers and lions as ____________________ animals, but they also have a soft and caring side.
9. Monsoon rains have caused the wood panels on my dining room floor to ____________________.
10. Julian is ____________________ to create a health clinic in Da Nang; if his vision materializes, he will have a flourishing health center in a few years.

Lesson 7

MAYORAL ADDRESS

Tomorrow afternoon, citizens will **convene** at City Hall and listen to the mayor's speech. The talk is especially important because the town has recently endured numerous problems: **harsh** rains, two fires, and a measles outbreak. It is expected that the mayor will be **articulate** in his oration, focusing on pragmatic solutions to the recent problems rather than lofty, **theoretical** issues. Hopefully his presentation will **blend** a sense of action together with a hope that, together, the community can overcome recent tribulations.

NEW WORDS

articulate
är'tikyəlit

harsh
härSH

blend
blend

convene
kən'vēn

theoretical
THēə'retikəl

Definitions: Try matching the words in the list with the appropriate definitions. If you are stuck, check the glossary in the back of the book or the passage at the top of the page.

1.	articulate	__________	a.	(adj.) having the ability to speak fluently and coherently; (v.) to express an idea or feeling fluently and coherently
2.	harsh	__________	b.	concerned with or involving the abstract ideas of a field or study rather than its practical application
3.	blend	__________	c.	(n.) a mixture of different things or qualities; (v.) to mix a substance with another so that they meld together as a mass; to put abstract things together; a harmonious combination
4.	convene	__________	d.	unpleasantly jarring to the senses or rough; cruel or severe
5.	theoretical	__________	e.	to come or bring together for a meeting or activity; to assemble

Sentences: Try to use the words above in a sentence below. Remember that a word ending may be changed or its figure of speech slightly altered.

6. The décor of the new bodega constitutes a(n) ____________________ of Spanish colonial imagery and California flora.
7. Grounding a child for a year for not doing homework seems ____________________.
8. Most professors have a solid grasp of ____________________ ideas in their field; many, however, cannot implement such ideas in the real world.
9. It is important for celebrities to be ____________________ about issues that impassion them, for a well-known voice can go a long way in helping implement change.
10. Educators will ____________________ at the resort hotel next week to discuss educational opportunities in the Pacific Rim.

NEW WORDS

antisocial
ˌantēˈsōSHəl, ˌantī-

raze
rāz

relish
ˈreliSH

caliber
ˈkaləbər

incur
inˈkər, iNG-

Lesson 8

THE LONER ARCHITECT

Jack is an architect of the highest **caliber**, as he possesses rare design talents, innovation, and creativity. However, others often do not **relish** his company. Often they find Jack's **antisocial** nature and condescending airs discomforting, and they do not wish to **incur** hostility stemming from unnecessary interactions with him. When state officials decided to **raze** the abandoned church — Jack's first and most memorable architectural project — for a public parking lot, some of Jack's coworkers feared his bitterness and quit their job because of it.

Definitions: Try matching the words in the list with the appropriate definitions. If you are stuck, check the glossary in the back of the book or the passage at the top of the page.

1.	antisocial	________	a.	to become subject to (something unwelcome or unpleasant) as a result of one's own behavior or actions
2.	raze	________	b.	to enjoy greatly
3.	relish	________	c.	1. the quality of someone's character or the level of someone's ability; 2. the internal diameter or bore of a gun barrel
4.	caliber	________	d.	1. not friendly; not wanting the company of others; 2. contrary to the laws and customs of society
5.	incur	________	e.	to completely destroy (a building, town, or other site)

Sentences: Try to use the words above in a sentence below. Remember that a word ending may be changed or its figure of speech slightly altered.

6. Only students of high ____________________ are admitted to the competitive preparatory school down the road.
7. Next week construction companies will ____________________ the dilapidated building across the street.
8. Jose ____________________ numerous late fees when he forgot to pay any of his bills on time.
9. Lolita's friends construed her isolation as a sign that she had become ____________________; in reality, she had hidden herself away to write a book.
10. I don't just enjoy eating a gooey chocolate chip cookie; I ____________________ it.

Lesson 9

THE COMPETITORS

In the morning, the club owner found **graphic** obscenities drawn all over the narrow corridor that provided the **egress** from the nightclub to the street. He knew that this **ignoble** act was **deliberate**. He was convinced that the perpetrators were not random club goers, but instead were professionals hired by his competition. From the moment he opened his club and attracted much of the other club's visitors, he knew that conflict with the neighboring establishment would be **imminent**.

NEW WORDS

deliberate
diˈlibərit (adj.); -ˌrāt (v.)

graphic
ˈgrafik

ignoble
igˈnōbəl

egress
ˈēˌgres

imminent
ˈimənənt

Definitions: Try matching the words in the list with the appropriate definitions. If you are stuck, check the glossary in the back of the book or the passage at the top of the page.

1.	deliberate	________	a.	about to happen
2.	graphic	________	b.	(adj.) 1. of or related to visual art; 2. giving a vivid picture with explicit detail; (n.) a pictorial item displayed on a screen or stored as data
3.	ignoble	________	c.	(adj.) done consciously and intentionally; (v.) engage in long and careful consideration
4.	egress	________	d.	not honorable in character or in purpose
5.	imminent	________	e.	an exit

Sentences: Try to use the words above in a sentence below. Remember that a word ending may be changed or its figure of speech slightly altered.

6. If you need to evacuate the building, the ____________________ point is located behind the stairwell to the right.
7. The movie *Pulp Fiction* (1994) is noted for its ____________________ scenes and intense plot.
8. The jury is ____________________ about whether the defendant is guilty of first-degree murder.
9. It is ____________________ for a ruler to maliciously kill his own honest and supportive citizens.
10. It seems that the announcement of a new pontiff is ____________________, as there is white smoke emanating from the Sistine chapel.

NEW WORDS

summit
ˈsəmit

extravagant
ikˈstravəgənt

candid
ˈkandid

mar
mär

alternate
ˈôltərˌnāt

Lesson 10

NEWFOUND APLOMB

The fashion designer had reached the **summit** of fame. As a result, he grew in self-confidence and his collections became more and more **extravagant**. Yet the designer's boss was not happy about the former's huge expenditures and thus gave the designer his **candid** opinion on the matter. Despite this criticism, tensions with his boss could not **mar** the designer's newfound confidence. He knew that his work had become very valuable in the market and that his boss could not easily find an **alternate** for him.

Definitions: Try matching the words in the list with the appropriate definitions. If you are stuck, check the glossary in the back of the book or the passage at the top of the page.

1.	summit	________	a.	truthful and straightforward; frank
2.	extravagant	________	b.	to impair the appearance, to disfigure; to impair the quality of
3.	candid	________	c.	1. the highest point of a hill or mountain; 2. a meeting between heads of government
4.	mar	________	d.	(adj.) 1. every other; every second; 2. taking the place of; (n.) a person who acts as a substitute; (v.) to occur in turn repeatedly
5.	alternate	________	e.	lacking restraint in spending money or resources; exceeding what is reasonable or appropriate

Sentences: Try to use the words above in a sentence below. Remember that a word ending may be changed or its figure of speech slightly altered.

6. Unlike Jake, who is superficial and fake, Corey is ____________________.
7. A climate change ____________________ will be held in Mexico City next month; leaders of many nations are expected to attend.
8. Because I want to save money, I do not live a(n) ____________________ lifestyle.
9. Do you have any ____________________ ideas if we are unable to travel to New Orleans for Mardi Gras?
10. The unruly teenager attempted to ____________________ his neighbor's reputation by saying mean things about her.

Crossword Puzzle

Lessons 1-10

ACROSS

6 (adj.) having a healthy red or reddish color; (v.) to make reddish in color
7 (n.) the expression of approval or admiration of someone or something; (v.) to express warm approval of
8 (v.) to become larger or stronger
10 (n.) the act of holding someone closely in one's arms; (v.) 1. to hold someone closely in one's arms; 2. to accept or support a belief, theory, or change willingly and enthusiastically; 3. to include or contain something as a constituent part
16 (adj.) concerned with or involving the abstract ideas of a field or study rather than its practical application
17 (adj.) 1. not friendly; not wanting the company of others; 2. contrary to the laws and customs of society
18 (adj.) unpleasantly jarring to the senses or rough; cruel or severe
19 (v.) to become subject to (something unwelcome or unpleasant) as a result of one's own behavior or actions
20 (adj.) about to happen

DOWN

1 (adj.) best or most favorable
2 (v.) (of sums of money or benefits) to be received by someone in regular or increasing amounts over time
3 (v.) to impair the appearance, to disfigure; to impair the quality of
4 (v.) to revive someone from unconscious or apparent death; to make an idea or enterprise vigorous again
5 (v.) 1. to handle or control (a tool, mechanism, etc.) in a skillful manner; to edit, alter, or move text or data on a computer; 2. to control or influence a person or situation cleverly, unscrupulously, or unfairly; to alter data or present statistics so as to mislead
9 (adj.) savagely fierce, cruel, or violent
11 (v.) to be quick to do something; to move hurriedly
12 (v.) to make a general or broad statement by inferring from specific cases; to make something more widespread or common
13 (n.) 1. the highest point of a hill or mountain; 2. a meeting between heads of government
14 (n.) a shine or luster on a smooth surface; (v.) to conceal or disguise something by treating it briefly or representing it misleadingly
15 (adj.) 1. of or related to visual art; 2. giving a vivid picture with explicit detail; (n.) a pictorial item displayed on a screen or stored as data

Vocabulary Review
Lessons 1 - 10

Directions: Match each word with its best approximate definition. Note that definitions are not necessarily repeated verbatim from the lesson exercises.

1.	fickle	_______	a.	wrong, false, incorrect
2.	diligent	_______	b.	having the ability to speak or to speak fluently and coherently
3.	noisome	_______	c.	a person or thing vital to an organization or enterprise
4.	beneficial	_______	d.	lacking restraint in spending money or resources
5.	celestial	_______	e.	a beggar
6.	enthrall	_______	f.	to capture the attention of and fascinate
7.	linchpin	_______	g.	positioned in or relating to the sky or heavens
8.	erroneous	_______	h.	occurring in limited numbers or quantities; insufficient for the demand
9.	lithe	_______	i.	having an offensive smell
10.	scarce	_______	j.	to completely destroy (a building or site)
11.	warp	_______	k.	showing care or conscientiousness in one's abilities
12.	mendicant	_______	l.	to bring together for a meeting or activity; to assemble
13.	articulate	_______	m.	truthful and straightforward; frank
14.	convene	_______	n.	thin, supple, graceful (concerning one's body)
15.	raze	_______	o.	to become or cause to become bent, usually as a result of dampness or heat
16.	relish	_______	p.	favorable or advantageous
17.	ignoble	_______	q.	an exit
18.	egress	_______	r.	to enjoy greatly
19.	extravagant	_______	s.	dishonorable in character or purpose
20.	candid	_______	t.	changing one's loyalties, interests, or affection frequently

Word Roots: Unit 1

ROOTS AND THEIR MEANINGS

hyper:	**over**	**fic/fig:**	**to make; to do**
epi:	**upon**	**vid/vis:**	**to see**
hypo:	**under**	**dem:**	**people**

Here are a few examples of some words that use the above roots:

hyperactive:	abnormally or extremely active
epidemic:	widespread occurrence of infectious disease in a community
hypothermia:	condition of having a low body temperature
figment:	something one believes to be real, but that he or she makes up in imagination
visual:	of or related to sight or seeing
demography:	the study of populations and changes in populations (especially as related to births, deaths, income, and disease)

Now try to fill in the table below by finding the appropriate root(s) and interpreting the meaning of each word:

Word	Root(s)	Guessed Meaning	Actual Meaning
hypersensitive			
video			
demographics			
hypothyroidism			
fictional			
epithet			
figurative			
epidermis			
hypertension			
figure (v.)			

NEW WORDS

variance
ˈve(ə)rēəns

vague
vāg

deficiency
diˈfiSHənsē

kiln
kiln, kil

reception
riˈsepSHən

Lesson 11

THE OLD BRICK MAKER

There was not much **variance** in the routine of the old brick maker. Every morning he put the new clay bricks in the **kiln** to bake and then laid them out in the yard to cool. His bricks always met with a warm **reception** – they were considered to be the best ones in the area. Recently, however, he began to feel a **vague** pain in his chest that made it harder to work. His doctor insisted that it was likely a vitamin **deficiency**, but the old brick maker felt that there was something wrong with his heart. With proper care, the old brick maker healed and continued his routine at his typical pace.

Definitions: Try matching the words in the list with the appropriate definitions. If you are stuck, check the glossary in the back of the book or the passage at the top of the page.

1.	variance	__________	a.	of uncertain, indefinite, or unclear character or meaning
2.	vague	__________	b.	the fact or quality of being different, divergent, or inconsistent
3.	deficiency	__________	c.	1. the action or process of receiving something sent, given, or inflicted; 2. a formal social occasion held to welcome someone or to celebrate a particular event; 3. the area in a hotel, office, or establishment where guests and visitors are greeted and dealt with
4.	kiln	__________	d.	a furnace or oven for burning, baking, or drying, especially one for firing pottery
5.	reception	__________	e.	a lack or shortage

Sentences: Try to use the words above in a sentence below. Remember that a word ending may be changed or its figure of speech slightly altered.

6. There is much ____________________ in how people interpret important novels.
7. I only have a(n) ____________________ idea of what I may be doing with my life twenty years from now.
8. After having made racist remarks, the journalist was welcomed at the annual banquet with a frigid ____________________.
9. Individuals with a reading ____________________ may experience difficulty comprehending prose or parsing the words contained in that prose.
10. When I took a pottery class last winter, Gary taught me how to use the ____________________ to fire my creations.

Lesson 12

KIDNAPPED

Frank woke up and found himself in the awful **predicament** of being kidnapped. He was able to **notice** only a locked door and a window in the room, the latter of which was big enough for him to climb through and escape. Yet, since Frank was chained up in shackles, he was not **ambulatory** and could not flee. After many hours of waiting, the **noxious** kidnapper finally entered to check on him. He threatened Frank to be obedient, and left a bowl of some **bland** soup behind. Frank quickly devoured the soup, but was unable to quench his anxiety about the future.

NEW WORDS

notice
ˈnōtis

noxious
ˈnäkSHəs

predicament
ˌənfôrˈsēn

bland
bland

ambulatory
ˈambyələˌtôrē

Definitions: Try matching the words in the list with the appropriate definitions. If you are stuck, check the glossary in the back of the book or the passage at the top of the page.

1.	notice	________	a.	a difficult, unpleasant, or embarrassing situation
2.	noxious	________	b.	lacking strong features or characteristics and therefore uninteresting; food or drink that is mild and insipid; a person lacking strong emotion and unremarkable
3.	predicament	________	c.	harmful, poisonous, or very unpleasant
4.	bland	________	d.	(n.) 1. attention, observation; 2. notification or warning of something, especially to allow preparations to be made; 3. a displayed sheet giving news or information; (v.) to become aware of
5.	ambulatory	________	e.	related to or adapted to walking

Sentences: Try to use the words above in a sentence below. Remember that a word ending may be changed or its figure of speech slightly altered.

6. Certain pesticides are ____________________ and thus have the potential to greatly erode human health.
7. After weeks of being practically bedridden, Sonya was finally ____________________ enough to walk to the grocery store.
8. It was hard not to ____________________ the orange stain that appeared on Natalie's white shirt this afternoon: she accidentally had spilled marinara sauce on her top at lunch.
9. Usually the Malaysian food at this restaurant is spicy, but today it seems to taste rather ____________________.
10. Jeremy found himself in a(n) ____________________ when his dissertation adviser passed away and there was nobody remaining who was capable of supervising his research.

Lesson 13

NEW WORDS

heirloom
ˈe(ə)rˌlo͞om

pose
pōz

pathetic
pəˈTHetik

instantaneous
ˌinstənˈtānēəs

forlorn
fərˈlôrn, fôr-

THE DISAPPOINTING WILL

James was convinced that he would inherit the old Chinese vase, which was his family's most valuable **heirloom**. He was **forlorn** when he found out that the vase was gifted to the local museum. When the estate lawyer finished reading the will, James' **instantaneous** reaction was to protest. He struck a **pose** of defiance; however, his **pathetic** effort to change the situation was completely futile.

Definitions: Try matching the words in the list with the appropriate definitions. If you are stuck, check the glossary in the back of the book or the passage at the top of the page.

1.	heirloom	________	a.	arousing pity, especially through vulnerability or sadness; miserable; inadequate
2.	pose	________	b.	(n.) 1. a way of standing or sitting, usually adopted in order to be photographed, drawn, or painted; 2. a particular way of behavior adopted in order to give others a false impression or to impress others; (v.) 1. to present or constitute (a problem, danger, or difficulty); 2. to assume a particular attitude in order to be photographed, drawn, or painted; 3. to behave affectedly in order to impress others
3.	pathetic	________	c.	occurring or done immediately
4.	instantaneous	________	d.	a valuable object that has belonged to a family for several generations
5.	forlorn	________	e.	pitifully sad, abandoned, or lonely; miserable; inadequate

Sentences: Try to use the words above in a sentence below. Remember that a word ending may be changed or its figure of speech slightly altered.

6. That necklace is a family ____________________ that belonged to my mother's parents.
7. Unlike in the nineteenth century, in the digital world communication between people living far away can occur almost ____________________.
8. Ike's attempt to ask Paloma out was ____________________: rather than addressing Paloma directly, he had his friends suggest that the two meet for tea because he was lonely.
9. Often reporters ____________________ questions to celebrities and leaders during major events.
10. Larry became ____________________ when he realized that his puppy ran away.

Lesson 14

BUSINESS NEGOTIATIONS

Negotiations between the two companies reached a critical **juncture.** There was a **tacit** agreement between the two that the current market could handle only one of them since their products were **akin**. According to the younger company, which had modeled its products on the older one, a merger would **suffice** to clear the situation. Representatives of the older company, however, felt that the younger company had violated copyright laws and needed to pay a large sum of money to its **predecessor**. The two companies squabbled for weeks before finally settling their differences and merging.

NEW WORDS

tacit
ˈtasit

akin
əˈkin

juncture
ˈjəNGkCHər

suffice
səˈfīs

predecessor
ˈpredəˌsesər, ˈprē-

Definitions: Try matching the words in the list with the appropriate definitions. If you are stuck, check the glossary in the back of the book or the passage at the top of the page.

1.	tacit	________	a.	to be enough or adequate; to meet the needs of
2.	akin	________	b.	a person who held a job or office before another; a thing that has been followed or replaced by another
3.	juncture	________	c.	understood or implied without being stated
4.	suffice	________	d.	a particular point in events or time; a place where things join
5.	predecessor	________	e.	of similar character

Sentences: Try to use the words above in a sentence below. Remember that a word ending may be changed or its figure of speech slightly altered.

6. Not voting in an election is ________________ to not caring about the political future of the country.
7. Though I prefer job candidates to have a physics degree, candidates holding a mathematics degree will also ________________.
8. One might argue that a typewriter is a ________________ of the modern word processor.
9. At this ________________, you have important decisions to make about your future, for they will dictate your future path in life.
10. Unlike Gordon, who talked endlessly about gun control, Felicia remained ________________ on the issue.

NEW WORDS

yield
yēld

bard
bärd

clone
klōn

repress
ri'pres

conspicuous
kən'spikyoo͞oəs

Lesson 15

A BARD IN LOVE

Though the **bard** typically enjoyed expressing poetic thoughts about the ladies he met, he quit doing so after he met Julia. Private and introverted by nature, Julia begged him not to publicize their relationship in his art or to **clone** the private love notes that he wrote to her. Though he **yielded** to her wishes, it was difficult for him to **repress** his feelings. And although Julia did not want people knowing about their relationship, their courtship became **conspicuous** after townsfolk saw the pair out dining together – the couple's privacy could not remain hidden forever.

Definitions: Try matching the words in the list with the appropriate definitions. If you are stuck, check the glossary in the back of the book or the passage at the top of the page.

1.	yield	________	a.	(n.) an identical copy of something; (v.) to make an identical copy of
2.	bard	________	b.	a poet, especially one conveying epics in an oral tradition
3.	clone	________	c.	to subdue someone or something by force; to restrain, prevent, or inhibit
4.	repress	________	d.	(n.) the full amount of an agricultural or industrial product; (v.) 1. to produce or provide; to generate; 2. to give way to arguments, demands, pressure, or traffic
5.	conspicuous	________	e.	standing out so as to be clearly visible

Sentences: Try to use the words above in a sentence below. Remember that a word ending may be changed or its figure of speech slightly altered.

6. This year our ____________________ of apples was over two thousand tons!
7. Dolly the sheep was the first living mammal to be ____________________.
8. It was ____________________ that the teacher did not prepare for class because he could not deliver the lecture without being completely dependent on his notes.
9. The eloquent ____________________ told the story of his kingdom in a melodramatic fashion.
10. It was hard for Michael to ____________________ his feelings at the funeral; he tried to hold back, but tears eventually flowed profusely from his eyes.

Lesson 16

THE TRUTH WILL OUT

The management style of the new science fiction film director was quite **erratic**. It resulted in chaos on the set, especially from the actors playing **galactic** warriors who spent hours each day getting made up as extraterrestrials for their roles. Such awful leadership resulted in **innumerable** contract details that needed to be resolved and an increasingly chaotic morale. Despite such bedlam, the director's prior employer did **vouch** for him: they said he had been their best director. They obviously had lied, and the new movie company's representatives simply stood **aghast** at the sight of the director's sheer incompetence.

NEW WORDS

erratic
iˈratik

galactic
gəˈlaktik

aghast
əˈgast

innumerable
iˈn(y)o͞omərəbəl

vouch
vouch

Definitions: Try matching the words in the list with the appropriate definitions. If you are stuck, check the glossary in the back of the book or the passage at the top of the page.

1.	erratic	__________	a.	filled with shock or horror
2.	galactic	__________	b.	of or relating to galaxies, especially the Milky Way
3.	aghast	__________	c.	too many to be counted (used often in exaggeration)
4.	innumerable	__________	d.	uneven in pattern or movement
5.	vouch	__________	e.	to assert or confirm from one's experience that something is true or accurately as described

Sentences: Try to use the words above in a sentence below. Remember that a word ending may be changed or its figure of speech slightly altered.

6. It is important to have others ____________________ for your character, accomplishments, and credibility when an employer solicits references.
7. Jacob's ____________________ attendance in class probably explains why his grades are not as high as they could be.
8. There are ____________________ grains of sand on that beach; one could never fathom counting them all.
9. The new movie provides viewers with a(n) ____________________ experience, showing them the vast star systems in the Milky Way.
10. Artie was ____________________ when he heard that someone had broken his favorite piano.

NEW WORDS

lore
lôr

tumult
't(y)oo͞ˌməlt

arbitrator
'ärbiˌtrātər

retract
ri'trakt

adroit
ə'droit

Lesson 17

AN ACT OF BETRAYAL

After acquiring the elixir – which could extend life according to traditional **lore** – from the chief of the Kanbu tribe, the King decided to **retract** his words. He refused to sign the peace treaty and concede part of his land to the tribe as he promised, inciting political **tumult**. An **arbitrator** was sent to settle the conflict, but his **adroit** persuasion still failed to appease the irate chief.

Definitions: Try matching the words in the list with the appropriate definitions. If you are stuck, check the glossary in the back of the book or the passage at the top of the page.

1.	lore	________	a.	an independent person or body officially appointed to settle a dispute
2.	tumult	________	b.	to draw or be drawn back in; withdraw
3.	arbitrator	________	c.	a body of traditions and knowledge on a subject or held by a particular group, typically transmitted by word of mouth
4.	retract	________	d.	a loud confused noise, especially one caused by a mass of people; confusion or disorder
5.	adroit	________	e.	clever or skillful in using the hands or mind

Sentences: Try to use the words above in a sentence below. Remember that a word ending may be changed or its figure of speech slightly altered.

6. Sitting in her apartment, Shaolaine heard the ________________ as protests broke out in the park.
7. According to Norse ________________, Thor is the god of thunder.
8. Colleen was so ________________ with her hands that she stole her friend's wallet without the latter even noticing.
9. When disputes become nasty, they often require a(n) ________________ to help resolve them.
10. Realizing that he had, perhaps, promised to deliver too much, Mark asked if he could ________________ his last offer in the business negotiation.

Lesson 18

BEHIND THE CURTAINS

The **merger** between the two theater companies was a task of **herculean** proportions. There was an **inclination** on both sides to resist cooperation. The companies' representatives responsible for the merger felt that there was no **antidote** to the inflated egos of the artists. Each of the two groups of actors would try to **abash** the other by sneering and making disparaging remarks during the meetings. The merger was doomed to fail from the beginning.

NEW WORDS

abash
əˈbaSH

antidote
ˈantiˌdōt

inclination
ˌinkləˈnāSHən, ˌiNGklə-

herculean
ˌhərkyəˈlēən, hərˈkyo͞olēən

merger
ˈmərjər

Definitions: Try matching the words in the list with the appropriate definitions. If you are stuck, check the glossary in the back of the book or the passage at the top of the page.

1.	abash	__________	a.	a medicine taken to counteract a particular poison
2.	antidote	__________	b.	requiring great strength or effort
3.	inclination	__________	c.	a combination of two things (usually companies) into one
4.	herculean	__________	d.	to cause to feel embarrassed, disconcerted, or ashamed
5.	merger	__________	e.	1. a person's natural tendency to act in a particular way; a propensity or disposition; 2. a slope or slant; 3. the angle at which a straight line or plane intersects another

Sentences: Try to use the words above in a sentence below. Remember that a word ending may be changed or its figure of speech slightly altered.

6. It was a(n) ____________________ task to move all of my stuff from my old house to my new one.
7. The ____________________ between the two companies will offer new business opportunities, but the employees from the respective companies must get along first.
8. Allegra felt ____________________ when her parents discussed her previous boyfriends with her fiancé and his family.
9. Often the best ____________________ for the common cold is a bowl of piping hot chicken soup.
10. Because I have little ____________________ to study robotics for months, I do not think I should be helping you build intelligent machines.

NEW WORDS

shirk
SHərk

pigment
ˈpigmənt

brevity
ˈbrevitē

conduit
ˈkänˌd(y)o͞oət, ˈkänd(w)ət

iniquity
iˈnikwitē

Lesson 19

ON OBTAINING A BLUE HUE

In Renaissance Italy, obtaining a deep blue **pigment** was a costly endeavor. This is because the stone providing this color – lapis lazuli – had to be transported from far away (present-day Afghanistan). Because the Renaissance era lacked modern transport, delivery of such stones was a process that lacked **brevity**. Access to merchants, of course, served as a main **conduit** through which such stones could eventually be obtained and delivered. But if a merchant was inclined to **shirk** his responsibility, such stones may never arrive and the purchaser would lose his or her money in the purchase. For this reason, selecting a merchant with credibility was very important, and any display of **iniquity** in the trading community was broadcast widely and could easily damage one's career.

Definitions: Try matching the words in the list with the appropriate definitions. If you are stuck, check the glossary in the back of the book or the passage at the top of the page.

1.	shirk	________	a.	to avoid or neglect a duty or responsibility
2.	pigment	________	b.	the natural coloring of plant or animal tissue; a substance used for coloring or painting, especially a dry powder that, when mixed with water or oil, forms a paint or ink
3.	brevity	________	c.	immoral or grossly unfair behavior
4.	conduit	________	d.	concise and exact use of words in speech; shortness of time
5.	iniquity	________	e.	a channel for conveying a fluid; a person or organization that acts as a channel for the transmission of something

Sentences: Try to use the words above in a sentence below. Remember that a word ending may be changed or its figure of speech slightly altered.

6. Only years of penitence could help mitigate the old man's ________________.
7. The ________________ for the red color in that painting comes from the stones that I bought in the market last week.
8. The Detroit River serves as a(n) ________________ that connects the larger bodies of water Lake Erie and Lake St. Clair.
9. Good writing should be praised not only for its clarity but also for its ________________: it is best to be eloquent in as few words as possible
10. If you ________________ your responsibilities, there may be negative repercussions.

Lesson 20

RALPH AND THE YACHT

When Ralph's parents agreed to **grant** him access to the family yacht after he graduated from college, a **priceless** expression of glee appeared on his face. Ralph had wanted to ride the yacht ever since he was six, and each year his family would **convey** to him that the boat was reserved only for adults. Finally old enough to travel himself, Ralph joyously guided the yacht out to sea for the first time. He found the **drone** of the boat's motor so relaxing that he fell asleep for hours. Twelve hours later he woke up stranded at sea in the middle of the night. He had to phone his family for help, and thus felt compelled to **prevaricate** about what had happened when pressed by his parents for an explanation.

NEW WORDS

grant
grant

priceless
ˈprīsləs

convey
kənˈvā

prevaricate
priˈvariˌkāt

drone
drōn

Definitions: Try matching the words in the list with the appropriate definitions. If you are stuck, check the glossary in the back of the book or the passage at the top of the page.

1.	grant	__________	a.	to speak or act in an evasive way
2.	priceless	__________	b.	so precious that its value cannot be determined
3.	convey	__________	c.	(n.) a sum of money given by an organization, especially a government, for a particular purpose; (v.) 1. to agree to give or allow (something requested) to; 2. to agree or admit to someone that something is true
4.	prevaricate	__________	d.	to transport or carry from place to place; to make an idea, impression, or feeling known or understandable to someone
5.	drone	__________	e.	(n.) a low, continuous humming sound; (v.) to make a continuous low humming sound; to speak tediously in a monotonous tone

Sentences: Try to use the words above in a sentence below. Remember that a word ending may be changed or its figure of speech slightly altered.

6. Often in fairy tales, a genie will ____________________ his or her master three wishes.
7. Stephanie shut the window to help drown out the ____________________ of the vehicle motors.
8. It was difficult for the lost child to ____________________ his gratitude to the strangers who helped reunite him with his parents.
9. While clothing, cars, and fine dining are costly, developing a relationship with your child is indeed a(n) ____________________ experience.
10. When asked about his business intentions, the lobbyist chose to ____________________ to the media about them.

Word Search

Lessons 11-20

L S V A R I A N C E N V S B
M D U D F E P C O N D U I T
V G R O C O T I G P O J E V
R A R I U S R N G E N L M X
B E T O A C T L N M B T K P
G O G H T N I A O A E I Y Q
N S G R A A T P R R L N J B
Y A U R E N R E S N N P T M
G E G F A M M T B N L M A R
L Z V T F U W N I L O B L D
N O S N N I I X N B A C G D
R N R N O K C V R S R N J K
I X I E A C X E H K X A D N

1 (n.) the fact or quality of being different, divergent, or inconsistent
2 (n.) a furnace or oven for burning, baking, or drying, especially one for firing pottery
3 (n.) 1. attention, observation; 2. notification or warning of something, especially to allow preparations to be made; 3. a displayed sheet giving news or information; (v.) to become aware of
4 (adj.) lacking strong features or characteristics and therefore uninteresting; food or drink that is mild and insipid; a person lacking strong emotion and unremarkable
5 (adj.) occurring or done immediately
6 (adj.) pitifully sad, abandoned, or lonely
7 (adj.) of similar character
8 (v.) to be enough or adequate; to meet the needs of
9 (n.) a poet, especially one conveying epics in an oral tradition
10 (adj.) standing out so as to be clearly visible
11 (adj.) filled with shock or horror
12 (adj.) too many to be counted (used often in exaggeration)
13 (n.) a body of traditions and knowledge on a subject or held by a particular group, typically transmitted by word of mouth
14 (n.) an independent person or body officially appointed to settle a dispute
15 (v.) to cause to feel embarrassed, disconcerted, or ashamed
16 (n.) a combination of two things (usually companies) into one
17 (n.) the natural coloring of plant or animal tissue; a substance used for coloring or painting, especially a dry powder that, when mixed with water or oil, forms a paint or ink
18 (n.) a channel for conveying a fluid; a person or organization that acts as a channel for the transmission of something
19 (n.) a sum of money given by an organization, especially a government, for a particular purpose; (v.) 1. to agree to give or allow (something requested) to; 2. to agree or admit to someone that something is true
20 (v.) to transport or carry from place to place; to make an idea, impression, or feeling known or understandable to someone

Vocabulary Review
Lessons 11-20

Directions: Match each word with its best approximate definition. Note that definitions are not necessarily repeated verbatim from the lesson exercises.

	Word			Definition
1.	vague	________	a.	a place where things join; a particular point in events or time
2.	deficiency	________	b.	loud confused noise typically caused by a mass of people; confusion or disorder
3.	predicament	________	c.	sinfulness; immoral behavior
4.	ambulatory	________	d.	concise and exact use of words in speech; shortness of time
5.	heirloom	________	e.	to speak or act in an evasive way
6.	pathetic	________	f.	relating to or adapted to walking
7.	tacit	________	g.	not even or regular in pattern or movement
8.	juncture	________	h.	to give way to arguments, demands or pressure; to produce or provide a natural or agricultural product
9.	yield	________	i.	so precious its value cannot be determined
10.	clone	________	j.	to make an identical copy; a person or thing that is an identical copy of another
11.	erratic	________	k.	a valuable object belonging to a family for several generations
12.	galactic	________	l.	medicine taken to counteract a poison
13.	tumult	________	m.	a difficult, embarrassing, or unpleasant situation
14.	adroit	________	n.	arousing pity, especially through sadness or vulnerability; miserable; inadequate
15.	antidote	________	o.	relating to galaxies, especially the Milky Way
16.	herculean	________	p.	requiring great strength or effort
17.	brevity	________	q.	clever in using the hands or mind
18.	iniquity	________	r.	implied or understood without being stated
19.	priceless	________	s.	a lack or shortage
20.	prevaricate	________	t.	uncertain or indefinite in character or meaning

Word Roots: Unit 2

ROOTS AND THEIR MEANINGS

pro:	**forward, supporting**	**pon/pos:**	**to put; to place**
eu:	**pleasing**	**voc:**	**to call**
sequ/secu:	**to follow**	**luc/lum:**	**light, bright**

Here are a few examples of some words that use the above roots:

proactive:	creating or controlling a situation by being active rather than passive after it has taken place
euphoric:	characterized by feeling of intense excitement and happiness
consequential:	following as a result or effect of something; important or substantive
deposit (v.):	to put or set down something (usually money) in a specific place, often for safekeeping
vocal:	expressing feelings loudly
luminous:	full of shedding light; very bright

Now try to fill in the table below by finding the appropriate root(s) and interpreting the meaning of each word:

Word	Root(s)	Guessed Meaning	Actual Meaning
sequence			
postpone			
lucid			
provocative			
deposit			
eulogy			
consecutive			

Lesson 21

THE ART HISTORY LECTURE

The teacher gave an **oration** in which she attempted to **illustrate** the value of Victorian art. She discussed the **detrimental** effects of social taboos on artistic expression during that time period. She cited the standard experts on Victorian art as well as some **additional** sources, which she found to be illustrative in proving her point. She explained to the students that many artists from that time period were considered **impudent** if their work was too sexually explicit for the conservative Victorian public.

NEW WORDS

illustrate
ˈiləˌstrāt

oration
ôˈrāSHən

additional
əˈdiSHənl

detrimental
ˌdetrəˈmentl

impudent
ˈimpyəd(ə)nt

Definitions: Try matching the words in the list with the appropriate definitions. If you are stuck, check the glossary in the back of the book or the passage at the top of the page.

1.	illustrate __________	a.	1. to provide (a book, newspaper, etc.) with pictures; 2. to explain or make something clear by way of charts, pictures, and other visuals; 3. to serve as an example of
2.	oration __________	b.	tending to cause harm
3.	additional __________	c.	not showing due respect for another person
4.	detrimental __________	d.	a formal speech, ordinarily one that is given on a ceremonial occasion
5.	impudent __________	e.	added, extra, or supplementary to what is already given

Sentences: Try to use the words above in a sentence below. Remember that a word ending may be changed or its figure of speech slightly altered.

6. The chairman's ____________________ was truly moving: his words inspired me to be a better worker.
7. Without someone to ____________________ my children's book, the text will be devoid of images to complement the text.
8. If anybody in the audience has ____________________ questions, such persons should feel free to contact me by email after the presentation.
9. Lack of exercise can be ____________________ to one's physical health and mental stability.
10. The ____________________ student castigated his teachers and walked out of school.

NEW WORDS

lexicon
ˈleksiˌkän, -kən

brusque
brəsk

paltry
ˈpôltrē

recognize
ˈrekigˌnīz, ˈrekə(g)ˌnīz

incoherent
ˌinkōˈhi(ə)rənt, ˌiNG-, -ˈher-

Lesson 22

GOING BACK TO THE VILLAGE

The old man was lying on the bed almost unconscious. Stephen listened to his **incoherent** mumble, trying to figure out what his father was saying. After so many years, he could only **recognize** some of the words in his father's **lexicon**, which was full of **brusque** and often offensive expressions typical of the local villagers. Stephen remembered why he left this village such a long time ago: everything about his father's farm, including his manner of speaking, struck him as **paltry** and outdated.

Definitions: Try matching the words in the list with the appropriate definitions. If you are stuck, check the glossary in the back of the book or the passage at the top of the page.

1.	lexicon	__________	a.	abrupt or offhand in speech or manner
2.	brusque	__________	b.	the vocabulary of a person, language, or branch of knowledge
3.	paltry	__________	c.	a small or meager amount of something; petty; trivial
4.	recognize	__________	d.	expressed in an incomprehensible or confusing way
5.	incoherent	__________	e.	1. to identify (someone or something) from having a previous encounter; 2. to acknowledge the existence, validity, or legality of

Sentences: Try to use the words above in a sentence below. Remember that a word ending may be changed or its figure of speech slightly altered.

6. Static on the telephone made my friend's words sound ____________________.
7. Nitya's ____________________ comments put off his sweet and caring girlfriend.
8. It was hard to ____________________ that the girl in the costume was actually my sister.
9. Though I speak fluent English, I am not well acquainted with the ____________________ of the shipping industry.
10. To work nine hours for a(n) ____________________ three dollars is exploitive.

Lesson 23

THE ART CUSTOMS OF AN ISLAND COMMUNITY

The **mores** of the island community encouraged artists to seek a wealthy **patron** to support their endeavors. Such values supported the **opinion** that artistic endeavors should be a spontaneous and **joyous** process and thus should not be influenced by an artist's monetary concerns. A patron could sponsor his or her favorite artist; however, the financial support also had to be within a reasonable **margin**. The community believed that the artist needed to remain humble and grounded as well if he or she was to produce authentic art.

NEW WORDS

patron
ˈpātrən

mores
ˈmôrˌāz

margin
ˈmärjən

opinion
əˈpinyən

joyous
ˈjoiəs

Definitions: Try matching the words in the list with the appropriate definitions. If you are stuck, check the glossary in the back of the book or the passage at the top of the page.

1.	patron	__________	a.	the fundamental customs and conventions of a community
2.	mores	__________	b.	a view or judgment formed about something, not necessarily based on fact or knowledge; a formal statement by an expert rendering advice or judgment on a matter
3.	margin	__________	c.	1. a person who gives financial support to another individual, a cause, an organization, or an activity; 2. a customer (typically a regular one)
4.	opinion	__________	d.	1. the edge or border of something; 2. the amount by which a thing is won or falls short
5.	joyous	__________	e.	full of happiness and excitement

Sentences: Try to use the words above in a sentence below. Remember that a word ending may be changed or its figure of speech slightly altered.

6. Often in seventeenth-century books, readers can find handwriting in the ____________________ of a page.
7. I am a special ____________________ of the Thai restaurant on the peninsula.
8. To a Westerner, some of the ____________________ of the Cambodian people seem quite alien.
9. Usually Christmas is a(n) ____________________ holiday for me, but for some reason I feel somewhat down this holiday season.
10. In my ____________________, students who do not do their homework do not deserve a tutor.

Lesson 24

NEW WORDS

scalpel
ˈskalpəl

goodwill
ˌgo͝odˈwil

gainsay
ˌgānˈsā, ˈgānˌsā

buffet
bəˈfā (n.); ˈbəfit (v.)

facile
ˈfasəl

NURTURE

Jim saw it as a gesture of **goodwill** to invite his students to a **buffet** before their final exam. No one on campus, in fact, could **gainsay** that Jim was one of the kindest mentors who always tried to **facilitate** a rapport between him and his students. Jim always knew that a good mentoring relationship entailed more than just pedagogy. Though he likened providing incisive analysis on student papers with his red pen to a surgeon operating with a **scalpel**, Jim made it a priority to be a supportive presence for his students in more ways than one.

Definitions: Try matching the words in the list with the appropriate definitions. If you are stuck, check the glossary in the back of the book or the passage at the top of the page.

1.	scalpel	________	a.	a surgical knife
2.	goodwill	________	b.	(n.) a meal consisting of several dishes in which guests serve themselves; (v.) to strike repeatedly; to batter; to knock someone over or off course
3.	gainsay	________	c.	easily achieved or effortless; superficial
4.	buffet	________	d.	friendly, helpful, or cooperative feelings or attitude
5.	facile	________	e.	to deny or contradict a fact or statement

Sentences: Try to use the words above in a sentence below. Remember that a word ending may be changed or its figure of speech slightly altered.

6. The defendant tried to ________________ the plaintiff's accusations with evidence and testimony.
7. On account of Marisa's ________________, she was given an internship at the local design studio.
8. The Sunday morning ________________ at the hotel is fabulous: I love the endless flow of drinks, carving station, and curry corner.
9. For a mathematician, adding numbers is a(n) ________________ task.
10. One cannot perform a successful operation if one does not have a(n) ________________ handy.

Lesson 25

THE SPENDTHRIFT SALES MANAGER

The sales manager sometimes made **frivolous** purchases. For instance, he had a weakness for purchasing **newfangled** gadgets that the company could do without. Yet despite these acquisitions, he was able to **operate** the business well and it make it a profit. This was primarily because he liked to **collaborate** with people from other departments. He was also quite **discreet** about his extravagant purchases. Overall, the CEO appreciated the sales manager's work, and the latter's unorthodox spending practices seemed not to undermine executive support for him.

NEW WORDS

discreet
disˈkrēt

newfangled
ˈn(y)o͞oˈfaNGgəld, -ˌfaNG-

collaborate
kəˈlabəˌrāt

frivolous
ˈfrivələs

operate
ˈäpəˌrāt

Definitions: Try matching the words in the list with the appropriate definitions. If you are stuck, check the glossary in the back of the book or the passage at the top of the page.

1.	discreet	_________	a.	to work jointly on an activity, especially to produce something
2.	newfangled	_________	b.	1. to control the functioning of a machine, process, or system; 2. to manage and run a business; 3. to perform a surgical procedure
3.	collaborate	_________	c.	not having any serious purpose or value
4.	frivolous	_________	d.	careful and circumspect in one's speech or actions, especially in order to avoid causing offense or to gain an advantage
5.	operate	_________	e.	different from what one is used to; objectionably new

Sentences: Try to use the words above in a sentence below. Remember that a word ending may be changed or its figure of speech slightly altered.

6. The ____________________ video game console allows players to experience virtual reality unlike any machine that came before it.
7. Bennett and Thao tried to be ____________________ about their relationship at work, for they did not want colleagues knowing that they were dating.
8. Going to the casino, to me, is not only a(n) ____________________ activity, but also a potentially dangerously expensive one, too.
9. I am learning how to ____________________ a crane so that I can become more experienced in construction.
10. Both professors are trying to ____________________ and write a history of Kazakhstan.

NEW WORDS

ascertain
ˌasərˈtān

evacuate
iˈvakyəˌwāt

objectionable
əbˈjekSHənəbəl

extol
ikˈstōl

solid
ˈsälid

Lesson 26

GABOR'S DOUBLE LIFE

Gabor had a **solid** reputation in his neighborhood. Everyone would look at him with admiration and **extol** him for all the free services he provided his neighbors through his company. This is why people did not find it **objectionable** when they did not see Gabor's children leave the house for days. No one suspected anything. However, a social worker visiting the house was immediately able to **ascertain** that the children looked very nervous and bothered. The social worker knew that she needed to **evacuate** the children from the house immediately and take them to a safe place in order to interrogate them.

Definitions: Try matching the words in the list with the appropriate definitions. If you are stuck, check the glossary in the back of the book or the passage at the top of the page.

1.	ascertain	________	a.	(adj.) 1. firm and stable in shape, not liquid or fluid; 2. not hollow; 3. dependable, reliable; (n.) a substance that is firm and stable in shape and not a liquid or fluid
2.	evacuate	________	b.	to find something out for certain; to make sure of
3.	objectionable	________	c.	arousing distaste or opposition; unpleasant or offensive
4.	extol	________	d.	to praise
5.	solid	________	e.	1. to remove someone (or several people) from a place of danger to a safe place; 2. to remove air, water, or other contents from a container

Sentences: Try to use the words above in a sentence below. Remember that a word ending may be changed or its figure of speech slightly altered.

6. After a conflagration broke out in the kitchen, the chef was forced to ____________________ the restaurant.
7. It is difficult to ____________________ the meaning of ancient Egyptian hieroglyphic texts.
8. If the student had received ____________________ support from his supervisors, he would not be struggling so much with his research.
9. I find Travis' behavior ____________________: he was rude to my parents and offended my little brother.
10. It is easy to ____________________ the virtues of America's founding fathers.

Lesson 27

THE WARRING SPOUSES

A weekend getaway with **splendid** views of the countryside was a promising **oasis** in their recently troubled marriage. Yet the husband seemed to be making a **unilateral** effort to save the marriage. His wife kept arguing with him during the trip, and their child served as a **buffer** between the warring couple. Whenever the husband pointed out that his wife simply did not want to cooperate, the wife would **repudiate** these claims and transfer the blame onto him.

NEW WORDS

splendid
ˈsplendid

oasis
ōˈāsis

buffer
ˈbəfər

unilateral
ˌyo͞onəˈlatərəl, -ˈlatrəl

repudiate
riˈpyo͞odēˌāt

Definitions: Try matching the words in the list with the appropriate definitions. If you are stuck, check the glossary in the back of the book or the passage at the top of the page.

1. splendid ________ a. to refuse to accept or be associated with; to deny the truth or validity of
2. oasis ________ b. 1. (of an action or decision) performed by or affecting only one person, group, or country involved in a particular situation, without the agreement of another or the others; 2. relating to, occurring on, or affecting only one side of an organ or structure, or of the body
3. buffer ________ c. (n.) a person or thing that prevents incompatible or antagonistic people or things from coming into contact with or harming each other; (v.) to lessen or moderate the impact of something
4. unilateral ________ d. a fertile spot in a desert where water is found
5. repudiate ________ e. magnificent; very impressive

Sentences: Try to use the words above in a sentence below. Remember that a word ending may be changed or its figure of speech slightly altered.

6. The caravan stopped at a(n) ____________________ to drink, bathe, and relax.
7. The St. Louis Gateway Arch is a(n) ____________________ monument: it provides an example of modern architecture and has a great view from the top.
8. Barry ____________________ every effort the girl made to ask him on a date.
9. It was a(n) ____________________ decision to expel the student who plagiarized his essay.
10. Jill erected a fence to serve as a(n) ____________________ between herself and her neighbor.

NEW WORDS

fanatic
fə'natik

copious
'kōpēəs

traumatic
trə'matik, trou-, trô-

effectual
i'fekCHo͞oəl

negative
'negətiv

Lesson 28

SHATTERED DREAMS

Max used to be a swimming **fanatic** who trained for hours each day and acquired **copious** medals for his talents. However, after a car crash damaged his vertebrae, swimming became an impossible task for Max. After visiting many hospitals, none offered an **effectual** remedy. The **traumatic** accident, as well as Max's realization that he might never be able to swim again, left Max with **negative** thoughts and some depression.

Definitions: Try matching the words in the list with the appropriate definitions. If you are stuck, check the glossary in the back of the book or the passage at the top of the page.

1.	fanatic	________	a.	emotionally disturbing or distressing
2.	copious	________	b.	(typically of something abstract or inanimate) successful in producing a desired or intended result; effective
3.	traumatic	________	c.	1. consisting in or characterized by the absence rather than the presence of distinguishing features; 2. not desirable or optimistic; 3. characterizing a number less than zero
4.	effectual	________	d.	abundant in supply or quantity
5.	negative	________	e.	a person filled with excessive single-minded passion, often for an extreme religious or political cause

Sentences: Try to use the words above in a sentence below. Remember that a word ending may be changed or its figure of speech slightly altered.

6. The court stenographer took ________________ notes during this morning's divorce trial.
7. Being mugged can be a(n) ________________ experience that takes some time and therapy to recover from.
8. The religious ________________ told the crowd that unless they became more spiritual immediately, they would all be damned.
9. Often ________________ people complain about everything and refuse to better themselves.
10. The law proved to be ________________ and, after its passing, women were granted suffrage rights.

Lesson 29

BECOMING INDEPENDENT

George's first company was a total **fiasco**. It went bankrupt in less than a year. Consequently, George's father employed him in his own company. The old man saw this as a **convenient** way to keep an eye on his son, who had become quite sullen and depressed. He knew George needed a daily **dose** of encouragement and support. Yet even though George seemed to be getting better, the memory of his failure remained as a **scourge** in his mind. George had always craved to see himself as a separate **entity** from his family, but he was still working for his father's business. This filled him with sadness and a quiet resolution to try and start a new company in the future.

NEW WORDS

convenient
kən'vēnyənt

fiasco
fē'askō

dose
dōs

entity
'entitē

scourge
skərj

Definitions: Try matching the words in the list with the appropriate definitions. If you are stuck, check the glossary in the back of the book or the passage at the top of the page.

1.	convenient	________	a.	a person or thing that causes great trouble or suffering
2.	fiasco	________	b.	a complete failure, usually in a ludicrous or humiliating way
3.	dose	________	c.	(n.) a quantity of a medicine or drug (or something analogous and unpleasant) recommended to be taken at a particular time; (v.) to administer a quantity of a medicine or drug to someone
4.	entity	________	d.	fitting in well with one's needs, activities, and/or plans
5.	scourge	________	e.	a thing with a distinct, independent existence

Sentences: Try to use the words above in a sentence below. Remember that a word ending may be changed or its figure of speech slightly altered.

6. For many Italians, Benito Mussolini (1883-1945) and his fascist regime was a(n) ____________________ upon democracy.
7. The Supreme Court is the highest legal ____________________ in the United States.
8. It is not ____________________ for me to drive across town just to deliver you one dollar.
9. A(n) ____________________ emerged as the waiter tripped and dropped the couple's dinner all over their clean clothing.
10. It is important to take a(n) ____________________ of your medicine every six hours to heal you from your infection.

NEW WORDS

rupture
ˈrəpCHər

vogue
vōg

strive
strīv

wan
wän

warrant
ˈwôrənt, ˈwä-

Lesson 30

TROUBLE AT THE PHARMACY

The police issued a **warrant** for the pharmacist's arrest, which caused a social **rupture** within the office. Half of his fellow pharmacists believed that their colleague was innocent, as his character seemed pure: he never would have sold medications on the black market. The rest of his fellow pharmacists were convinced that he was guilty, as his **wan** complexion at the sight of the cops intimated wrongdoing. Nevertheless, fellow coworkers' feelings ran so deep that both sides had to **strive** to make the pharmacy succeed amidst these legal troubles. Only the hope of running an organized office and carrying **vogue** medications bound the pharmacy team together.

Definitions: Try matching the words in the list with the appropriate definitions. If you are stuck, check the glossary in the back of the book or the passage at the top of the page.

1.	rupture	__________	a.	(usually of a pipe, vessel, or bodily organ) to break or burst suddenly
2.	vogue	__________	b.	(of skin) pale and weak, giving the impression of illness or exhaustion
3.	strive	__________	c.	(n.) a document issued by a legal or government official authorizing the police or some other body to make an arrest, search premises, or execute some other action to carry out justice; (v.) to justify or necessitate course of action
4.	wan	__________	d.	to make great efforts to achieve or obtain something
5.	warrant	__________	e.	(adj.) popular; fashionable; (n.) the prevailing fashion or style at a particular time

Sentences: Try to use the words above in a sentence below. Remember that a word ending may be changed or its figure of speech slightly altered.

6. After obtaining a(n) ____________________, the detective entered the suspect's home to search for the murder weapon.
7. It is important to ____________________ for your goals: without effort and hard work, it is hard to accomplish great things.
8. When the pipe ____________________ last week, sewage spilled all over the street.
9. During the 1950s, the hula hoop was in ____________________ internationally.
10. Eva's ____________________ complexion made me wonder whether she might be ill.

Crossword Puzzle

Lessons 21-30

ACROSS

2 (n.) a complete failure, usually in a ludicrous or humiliating way
4 (n.) a person or thing that causes great trouble or suffering
7 (n.) friendly, helpful, or cooperative feelings or attitude
10 (adj.) (of skin) pale and weak, giving the impression of illness or exhaustion
11 (adj.) abrupt or offhand in speech or manner
12 (v.) 1. to control the functioning of a machine, process, or system; 2. to manage and run a business; 3. to perform a surgery
14 (adj.) 1. (of an action or decision) performed by or affecting only one person, group, or country involved in a particular situation, without the agreement of another or the others; 2. relating to, occurring on, or affecting only one side of an organ or structure, or of the body.
15 (adj.) (typically of something abstract or inanimate) successful in producing a desired or intended result; effective
16 (adj.) expressed in an incomprehensible or confusing way
19 (adj.) tending to cause harm
20 (adj.) emotionally disturbing or distressing

DOWN

1 (adj.) full of happiness and excitement
3 (adj.) popular; fashionable; (n.) the prevailing fashion or style at a particular time
5 (v.) to refuse to accept or be associate with; to deny the truth or validity of
6 (adj.) easily achieved or effortless
8 (adj.) arousing distaste or opposition; unpleasant or offensive
9 (n.) a formal speech, ordinarily one that is given on a ceremonial occasion
13 (adj.) different from what one is used to; objectionably new
17 (n.) 1. a person who gives financial support to another individual, a cause, an organization, or an activity; 2. a customer (typically a regular one)
18 (v.) to find something out for certain; to make sure of

Vocabulary Review
Lessons 21-30

Directions: Match each word with its best approximate definition. Note that definitions are not necessarily repeated verbatim from the lesson exercises.

1.	additional	________	a.	abundant in quantity or supply
2.	impudent	________	b.	not containing serious value or purpose
3.	lexicon	________	c.	to praise enthusiastically
4.	paltry	________	d.	a person with excessive zeal for something
5.	mores	________	e.	(of a pipe, vessel, or other body part) to break or burst suddenly
6.	margin	________	f.	to deny or contradict a statement
7.	scalpel	________	g.	the edges or border of something
8.	gainsay	________	h.	to work jointly on an activity, typically to create something
9.	collaborate	________	i.	a surgical knife
10.	frivolous	________	j.	vocabulary of a person, language, or field
11.	evacuate	________	k.	to remove (a person) from a place of danger to a safe spot
12.	extol	________	l.	fitting well with one's needs, plans, or activities
13.	splendid	________	m.	added, extra, or supplementary to what is present or available
14.	oasis	________	n.	not showing respect for another
15.	fanatic	________	o.	a thing with a distinct and independent existence
16.	copious	________	p.	a spot on the desert that is fertile and where water is found
17.	convenient	________	q.	the essential characteristic customs of a community
18.	entity	________	r.	magnificent or very impressive
19.	rupture	________	s.	to take great efforts to achieve or attain something
20.	strive	________	t.	small or meager (of an amount)

Word Roots: Unit 3

ROOTS AND THEIR MEANINGS

her/hes:	**to stick**	**tract:**	**to drag, pull draw**
scrib/script:	**to write**	**port:**	**to carry**
mut:	**to change**	**ven/vent:**	**to come**

Here are a few examples of some words that use the above roots:

cohesive:	the quality of sticking together or forming a united whole
scripted:	something written out and then enacted
mutate:	to change or cause to change in form
retract:	to draw or be pulled back in; to withdraw
transport:	to move from one place to another by means of a vehicle
invent:	to create or design (to come upon) an idea

Now try to fill in the table below by finding the appropriate root(s) and interpreting the meaning of each word:

Word	Root(s)	Guessed Meaning	Actual Meaning
immutable			
coherent			
airport			
traction			
convene			
prescribe			
scribal			
portal			

NEW WORDS

shrewd
SHro͞od

scour
skou(ə)r

pompous
ˈpämpəs

ingenious
inˈjēnyəs

incision
inˈsiZHən

Lesson 31

AMAZING VETERINARIAN

William is an accomplished veterinarian who, on many occasions in his career, demonstrated how **shrewd** and sophisticated he was. Remember that **ingenious incision** he made to save a pregnant cow that had been swallowed whole by a python? A less savvy doctor would have chosen to chop up the snake, but William disregarded his older colleagues' **pompous** claims that he was wasting his time. He quickly got to work and made a long incision in the snake. He then extracted the cow and proceeded to **scour** the latter with hydrogen peroxide. Finally, he performed another operation – this time on the cow – and extracted a perfectly healthy calf. It was truly a remarkable feat.

Definitions: Try matching the words in the list with the appropriate definitions. If you are stuck, check the glossary in the back of the book or the passage at the top of the page.

1. shrewd ________ a. (n.) the action of cleaning or brightening the surface of something by rubbing it hard, typically with an abrasive or a detergent; (v.) to clean or brighten the surface of something by rubbing it hard, typically with an abrasive or a detergent; 2. to subject a place or text to a thorough search in order to try to locate something
2. scour ________ b. affectedly and irritatingly self-important or grand
3. pompous ________ c. having or showing sharp powers of judgment; astute
4. ingenious ________ d. a surgical cut made into the skin or flesh
5. incision ________ e. clever, original, and inventive

Sentences: Try to use the words above in a sentence below. Remember that a word ending may be changed or its figure of speech slightly altered.

6. The surgeon made a(n) ____________________ into the patient's stomach during the surgery.
7. An intelligent person who is ____________________ is a real turnoff; I much prefer smart individuals who are humble about their abilities.
8. The maid ____________________ the bathtub until it was clean and sparkly.
9. Placing electrical cords along the restaurant wall for customers to charge their electronic equipment is a(n) ____________________ idea.
10. Sometimes entrepreneurs must be ____________________ and manipulate people in order to create revenue for their company.

Lesson 32

THE LIFE CHANGING DECISION

Jacob eventually got tired of performing **menial** jobs and decided to go in **pursuit** of a higher education degree that would allow him to find a stable career. His **fidelity** to the family tradition of working in restaurants had kept him from realizing his potential for too long. He had always let the desire to please his parents **usurp** his own feelings about what he wanted to do. Moreover, working in restaurants for so many years had turned him into a **gourmand** and he needed to get out of that environment for health reasons as well. Now he was going to make changes in his life.

NEW WORDS

gourmand
go͝or'mänd

fidelity
fə'delətē

menial
'mēnēəl

pursuit
pər'so͞ot

usurp
yo͞o'sərp

Definitions: Try matching the words in the list with the appropriate definitions. If you are stuck, check the glossary in the back of the book or the passage at the top of the page.

1. gourmand ________ a. the act of following or chasing someone or something
2. fidelity ________ b. (of work) not requiring much skill and of little prestige
3. menial ________ c. faithfulness to a person, cause, or belief as exhibited by continuing loyalty and support; faithfulness to a spouse
4. pursuit ________ d. one who enjoys eating and who often eats too much
5. usurp ________ e. to take a position of power or importance illegally or by force

Sentences: Try to use the words above in a sentence below. Remember that a word ending may be changed or its figure of speech slightly altered.

6. For someone with a doctorate, having a career of cleaning toilets may feel like a(n) ________________ career.
7. Those who spend their entire lives in ________________ of happiness may never actually obtain it.
8. Lack of ________________ in a marriage can lead to serious problems, even divorce.
9. The insurgents tried to ________________ power from the established leadership.
10. Jo is such a ________________: she delights in food and all cuisines and typically stuffs her face.

NEW WORDS

acquiesce
ˌakwēˈes

choreography
ˌkôrēˈägrəfē

grovel
ˈgrävəl, ˈgrə-

laceration
ˌlasəˈrāSHən

incorrigible
inˈkôrijəbəl, -ˈkär-

Lesson 33

FOR THE SAKE OF ART

The new theater director's daring **choreography** included dancing around real pieces of broken glass. Anne knew that this would increase the dramatic effect in the play; however, she was well aware that a piece of glass could cause a **laceration** of the dancers' feet, especially when they had to **grovel** on the ground in part of the act. Unfortunately, the director had an **incorrigible** interest in dangerous stunts and Anne simply had to **acquiesce** to his decision. After all, he was much more famous and powerful than her.

Definitions: Try matching the words in the list with the appropriate definitions. If you are stuck, check the glossary in the back of the book or the passage at the top of the page.

1.	acquiesce ________		a.	a deep cut in the skin or flesh
2.	choreography ________		b.	the sequence of steps and movements in dance or figure skating
3.	grovel ________		c.	to accept something reluctantly and without protest
4.	laceration ________		d.	(of a person or his or her tendencies) unable to be corrected, reformed, or improved
5.	incorrigible ________		e.	to lie or move abjectly on the ground with one's face downward

Sentences: Try to use the words above in a sentence below. Remember that a word ending may be changed or its figure of speech slightly altered.

6. After hours of trying to persuade Danya to go to Hawaii with me, she finally ____________________.
7. The ____________________ behind that dance routine is genius: I love the sounds and rhythms involved.
8. Often a smoking habit is a(n) ____________________ habit, and people continue to smoke until they die.
9. I never knew that Shri had a(n) ____________________ on her back until I saw her in a swimsuit.
10. The dictator forced his subjects to ____________________ whenever they needed his approval for something.

Lesson 34

THE MYSTERIOUS STRANGER

The gypsy **nomad** was wearing a gorgeous red **frock** that took Lionel's breath away. Pleasant music was coming out of a strange **appliance** on the floor near her that looked like a hand-made radio. As the gypsy gracefully danced to the music, her movements created a deep feeling of **euphoria** in Lionel. He wondered if the girl was married. Listening to the sound of the music and watching the beautiful girl dance, for a moment Lionel forgot all about the world and any **atrocity** that had derailed his life.

NEW WORDS

atrocity
əˈträsitē

appliance
əˈplīəns

euphoria
yo͞oˈfôrēə

frock
fräk

nomad
ˈnōˌmad

Definitions: Try matching the words in the list with the appropriate definitions. If you are stuck, check the glossary in the back of the book or the passage at the top of the page.

1.	atrocity	__________	a.	an extremely wicked or cruel act, often involving physical violence or injury
2.	appliance	__________	b.	a feeling or state of intense happiness or excitement
3.	euphoria	__________	c.	a device or piece of equipment designed to perform a specific task, typically a domestic one
4.	frock	__________	d.	a woman's dress
5.	nomad	__________	e.	a person or a member of a people who travel from place to place

Sentences: Try to use the words above in a sentence below. Remember that a word ending may be changed or its figure of speech slightly altered.

6. A refrigerator is a necessary ____________________ for any modern kitchen.
7. It is a(n) ____________________ to burn a flag.
8. After Hattie won the lottery she was in a state of ____________________.
9. If you want my honest opinion, that ____________________ does not suit Erin very well.
10. After thirty years of working a desk job, Irving packed his bag to become a(n) ____________________ and explore the world

NEW WORDS

memento
məˈmenˌtō

illegible
i(l)ˈlejəbəl

migrate
ˈmīˌgrāt

rendezvous
ˈrändiˌvo͞o, -dā-

detour
ˈdēˌto͝or

Lesson 35

THE NEVER FORGOTTEN PAST

Jackson had kept one letter from his former fiancée as a **memento** of their love. After years of carrying it in his wallet, the letter had become almost **illegible**. A decade ago, when he had to **migrate** to another continent, he left the girl behind. Since then, whenever he returned to his home country, he would always take a **detour** to avoid her hometown. He was terrified at the prospect of a chance **rendezvous** with her. He could not bear the thought of looking into her eyes and experiencing feelings of guilt and remorse for leaving without her.

Definitions: Try matching the words in the list with the appropriate definitions. If you are stuck, check the glossary in the back of the book or the passage at the top of the page.

1.	memento	________	a.	an object kept as a reminder or souvenir of a person or event
2.	illegible	________	b.	a meeting at a specific time and place (typically between two people)
3.	migrate	________	c.	not clear enough to be read
4.	rendezvous	________	d.	(n.) a long and roundabout route taken to avoid something or to visit somewhere along the way; (v.) to take a long or roundabout route
5.	detour	________	e.	to move from one region or habitat to another (often seasonally); to move from one country to another; to move from one part of something to another

Sentences: Try to use the words above in a sentence below. Remember that a word ending may be changed or its figure of speech slightly altered.

6. Because of the highway construction, drivers were forced to take a thirty-mile ____________________ through Connecticut's suburbs.
7. That photograph of my mother is the only ____________________ I still have of my childhood.
8. The archivist had great difficulty trying to discern the ____________________ handwriting of the letters of French polymath Pierre Gassendi (1592-1655).
9. Anthropologists believe that humans ____________________ from Asia to North America across what is now the Bering Strait approximately 15,000 years ago.
10. The crab shack at the end of the road is a favorite ____________________ of Gene and his girlfriend.

Lesson 36

A MATTER OF PRINCIPLE

The mayor's office offered to give a **subsidy** to the NGO for cleaning up the city parks. To its surprise, NGO representatives were quick to **rebuff** the proposal. The NGO refused to work with the mayor, who had previously shown support for **malevolent** racist organizations and who had spoken with **levity** about serious issues such as the growing homelessness in the town. According to the NGO representatives, to work with this mayor would have been a **blasphemy** towards everything that the NGO stood for: after all, it was an organization fully dedicated to social justice and helping the poor.

NEW WORDS

malevolent
məˈlevələnt

blasphemy
ˈblasfəmē

levity
ˈlevətē

subsidy
ˈsəbsidē

rebuff
riˈbəf

Definitions: Try matching the words in the list with the appropriate definitions. If you are stuck, check the glossary in the back of the book or the passage at the top of the page.

1.	malevolent	__________	a.	to reject someone or something in an abrupt or ungracious manner
2.	blasphemy	__________	b.	the act of speaking sacrilegiously about God or things that are sacred
3.	levity	__________	c.	having a desire to harm or do evil to others
4.	subsidy	__________	d.	a sum of money granted by the government or a public body to assist an industry or business so that the price of a commodity will remain affordable
5.	rebuff	__________	e.	humor or frivolity; often treating a serious matter in a manner lacking due respect

Sentences: Try to use the words above in a sentence below. Remember that a word ending may be changed or its figure of speech slightly altered.

6. It is ____________________ against the Hindu religion to eat beef, as cows are considered sacred.
7. The ____________________ witch tried to poison the princess in an attempt to gain power over the kingdom.
8. The narcissistic dowager ____________________ the young man's attempts to secure a date with her.
9. Often students receive a(n) ____________________ from the government to assist them with their studies.
10. I miss my childhood, for it was a time of ____________________ when I had few worries in life.

NEW WORDS

flabbergast
'flabər,gast

clash
klaSH

idiom
'idēəm

fling
fliNG

famine
'famən

Lesson 37

LIFE'S TRIALS AND TRIBULATIONS

The way his sudden outbursts of aggression would **clash** with his usual cheerfulness was something that indeed did **flabbergast** her. When he was angry he would **fling** objects across the room, which scared her. Also, he would utter an **idiom** in his native language that she found very vulgar. Perhaps the recent **famine** in the region, which came as a result of a period of severe drought, had greatly unnerved him. Still, it could not justify his unacceptable behavior.

Definitions: Try matching the words in the list with the appropriate definitions. If you are stuck, check the glossary in the back of the book or the passage at the top of the page.

1.	flabbergast	________	a.	to greatly surprise someone, to astonish
2.	clash	________	b.	an extreme scarcity of food
3.	idiom	________	c.	a group of words having an established meaning that is not deducible from the words themselves
4.	fling	________	d.	(n.) a short period of enjoyment or wild behavior; (v.) to throw or hurl forcefully
5.	famine	________	e.	1. a violent confrontation; 2. a color mismatch; 3. a loud, jarring sound made by clashing metal objects together

Sentences: Try to use the words above in a sentence below. Remember that a word ending may be changed or its figure of speech slightly altered.

6. I was ____________________ when I arrived home from a long day's work only to find that my wife had cooked me a lovely meal.
7. "Going postal" is a(n) ____________________ that refers to going completely crazy, often to the point of harming innocent bystanders in one's way.
8. The objective of the game is to ____________________ a ring onto a stick.
9. Last year's ____________________ resulted in the death of over six hundred undernourished children.
10. The secretary and treasurer have personalities that ____________________: they cannot be together for more than ten minutes without getting into an explosive argument.

Lesson 38

THE HOMELESS BELIEVER

Joseph had a **constant**, unwavering faith in his church. Whenever life on the street became too challenging, he would **cling** to his faith. He kept a small icon in a **cavity** in the wall by his bed. Whenever one of the other homeless people in the shelter would **ruffle** him, Joseph took out the icon and would talk to in in a low voice. He loved Christmas best of all: on that day, a huge crowd of people would **amass** in his church and for that one day Joseph felt as if he was not alone in the world.

NEW WORDS

constant
ˈkänstənt

cling
kliNG

cavity
ˈkavitē

ruffle
ˈrəfəl

amass
əˈmas

Definitions: Try matching the words in the list with the appropriate definitions. If you are stuck, check the glossary in the back of the book or the passage at the top of the page.

1.	constant	________	a.	continuous and unchanging; remaining the same over a period of time; referring to a person who is faithful
2.	cling	________	b.	to gather together or accumulate over a time period; to gather together in a group or crowd
3.	cavity	________	c.	an empty space within a solid object, especially the human body; the decayed part of a tooth
4.	ruffle	________	d.	to hold on tightly to; to remain stubbornly persistent or faithful to something
5.	amass	________	e.	to disturb the smoothness or tranquility of; to disorder or disarrange

Sentences: Try to use the words above in a sentence below. Remember that a word ending may be changed or its figure of speech slightly altered.

6. In order to have an early retirement, it is wise to ____________________ as much money as possible at a young age and to invest it carefully.
7. A sinkhole is a giant ____________________ that opens up in the earth.
8. Janie was ____________________ by the insults that her family hurled at her last night.
9. The infant's ____________________ crying caused me to get up and leave the theater.
10. Even though evidence proved otherwise, the mother still wanted to ____________________ to the notion that her child was not a criminal.

Lesson 39

NEW WORDS

prior
ˈprīər

despondent
diˈspändənt

policy
ˈpäləsē

protrude
prəˈtro͞od, prō-

amorphous
əˈmôrfəs

INSENSITIVE MAYOR

After the new mayor was elected into office, many of the city's financially struggling citizens felt **despondent**. **Prior** to the mayoral election, the city had ample facilities in place to help those in need, but now under new leadership such plans suddenly seemed **amorphous**. This was because the new mayor vowed to implement a **policy** that would reduce the number of soup kitchens and homeless shelters around town. Moreover, he hoped to erect a large dock that would **protrude** from the city wharf; from here, those who could not afford food and housing would be exiled to nearby islands. What an insensitive new leader!

Definitions: Try matching the words in the list with the appropriate definitions. If you are stuck, check the glossary in the back of the book or the passage at the top of the page.

1. prior __________ a. without a clearly defined shape or form; vaguely defined
2. despondent __________ b. in low spirits from loss of hope or courage
3. policy __________ c. existing or occurring before in time, order, or importance
4. protrude __________ d. a course or principle of action adopted or proposed by a government, party, business, or individual
5. amorphous __________ e. to extend beyond or above a surface

Sentences: Try to use the words above in a sentence below. Remember that a word ending may be changed or its figure of speech slightly altered.

6. After being fired from her job without cause, Cameron felt ____________________.
7. The American Revolutionary War (1775-83) occurred ____________________ to the American Civil War (1861-65).
8. It is the school's ____________________ to prevent students from dropping classes beyond the fourth Tuesday of the semester.
9. Water is a(n) ____________________ entity, thus taking the form of any receptacle that contains it.
10. The cliff ____________________ into the ocean and provides tourists with a panoramic view of the seas.

Lesson 40

THE WAY THINGS ARE

In order to receive permission to fly, Johnson only needed written **approval** of the appointed psychologist. He entered the psychologist's office and saw a **portly** gentleman who was sweating profusely. The gentleman had a **fretful** look on his face as if something was bothering him. Johnson immediately knew from the man's face as well as from the **ominous** tone of his voice that there was going to be a problem obtaining the man's permission. Requiring a bribe to obtain approval documents was a **prevalent** practice in that town, and Johnson had prepared a large sum of money that he carried in his pocket for that purpose.

NEW WORDS

portly
ˈpôrtlē

approval
əˈpro͞ovəl

fretful
ˈfretfəl

ominous
ˈämənəs

prevalent
ˈprevələnt

Definitions: Try matching the words in the list with the appropriate definitions. If you are stuck, check the glossary in the back of the book or the passage at the top of the page.

1.	portly	__________	a.	feeling or expressing distress or irritation
2.	approval	__________	b.	giving the impression that something bad or unpleasant is about to happen
3.	fretful	__________	c.	stout or fat (usually in reference to a man)
4.	ominous	__________	d.	widespread over a particular area or at a particular time
5.	prevalent	__________	e.	the action of officially agreeing on something or accepting something as satisfactory

Sentences: Try to use the words above in a sentence below. Remember that a word ending may be changed or its figure of speech slightly altered.

6. Despite having received a(n) ____________________ warning from her mother not to go to the arcade at night, Sharon still went.
7. Christmas trees are ____________________ in many American suburbs during December.
8. The ____________________ bellhop carried the knapsack over his stout body and delivered it to the hotel room.
9. Kramer was ____________________ after the publisher rejected his book manuscript.
10. Children are allowed to go on the field trip to the water park only if they have obtained ____________________ from their parents.

Word Search

Lessons 31-40

```
T S B B M Q L E M E Y I L L T M
N U T L T E L U C G N J F Y N B
E O I L A F M N F C K I V I Y G
D P U E F S A E I T D Z N B W J
N M S U T I P S N E E C L I N G
O O R Q L A I H L T O R A Z M N
P P U P P O R I E R O M F L R N
S G P L N B T G R M O R A Y G L
E A R L N Y T I I R Y V D E M N
D K C O R F G R P M O I N C D R
M R B N V I N H J R S I L J L M
Z D J M B E O X P B M A X B Z N
Y J L L Q U L P U A S Q T D J D
W V E M S T A S F H D Q P R R J
```

1 (adj.) affectedly and irritatingly self-important or grand
2 (n.) a surgical cut made into the skin or flesh
3 (n.) faithfulness to a person, cause, or belief as exhibited by continuing loyalty and support; faithfulness to a spouse
4 (n.) the act of following or chasing someone or something
5 (v.) to lie or move abjectly on the ground with one's face downward
6 (adj.) (of a person or his or her tendencies) unable to be corrected, reformed, or improved
7 (n.) a device or piece of equipment designed to perform a specific task, typically a domestic one
8 (n.) a woman's dress
9 (n.) an object kept as a reminder or souvenir of a person or event
10 (v.) to move from one region or habitat to another (often seasonally); to move from one country to another; to move from one part of something to another
11 (n.) the act of speaking sacrilegiously about God or things that are sacred
12 (n.) a sum of money granted by the government or a public body to assist an industry or business so that the price of a commodity will remain affordable
13 (n.) 1. a violent confrontation; 2. a color mismatch; 3. a loud, jarring sound made by clashing metal objects together
14 (n.) an extreme scarcity of food
15 (v.) to hold on tightly to; to remain stubbornly persistent or faithful to something
16 (v.) to disturb the smoothness or tranquility of; to disorder or disarrange
17 (adj.) in low spirits from loss of hope or courage
18 (adj.) without a clearly defined shape or form; vaguely defined
19 (n.) the action of officially agreeing on something or accepting something as satisfactory
20 (adj.) feeling or expressing distress or irritation

Vocabulary Review
Lessons 31-40

Directions: Match each word with its best approximate definition. Note that definitions are not necessarily repeated verbatim from the lesson exercises.

	Word			Definition
1.	shrewd	________	a.	concerning work that requires little skill and lacks prestige
2.	ingenious	________	b.	to extend above or beyond a surface
3.	gourmand	________	c.	widespread in a particular area or at a particular time
4.	menial	________	d.	exhibiting sharp powers of judgment; astute
5.	acquiesce	________	e.	occurring continuously over a long time; unchanging
6.	laceration	________	f.	an extremely cruel act, often involving injury
7.	atrocity	________	g.	a feeling of intense excitement or happiness
8.	euphoria	________	h.	a deep cut in the skin
9.	illegible	________	i.	inventive, clever, original (of a person)
10.	detour	________	j.	to surprise someone greatly; to astonish
11.	malevolent	________	k.	giving the impression that something bad or unpleasant may happen
12.	rebuff	________	l.	to reject someone or something ungraciously
13.	flabbergast	________	m.	exhibiting a desire to harm others
14.	idiom	________	n.	a long roundabout route taken to avoid something or to visit somewhere along the way
15.	constant	________	o.	a person who enjoys eating and who often eats too much
16.	amass	________	p.	to gather together or accumulate
17.	prior	________	q.	to accept something reluctantly and without protest
18.	protrude	________	r.	not clear enough to be read
19.	ominous	________	s.	a group of words whose meaning cannot be deduced from the individual words alone
20.	prevalent	________	t.	existing before in time, order, or importance

Word Roots: Unit 4

ROOTS AND THEIR MEANINGS

man:	**hand**	**dic:**	**to say, tell**
clu/clo/cla:	**to shut**	**anim:**	**life, spirit**
ten:	**hold, keep**	**esce:**	**to become**

Here are a few examples of some words that use the above roots:

manual:	done by hand; a handbook of instructions for learning to operate something
cloister:	a convent or monastery (a place where one is shut up and shielded from the world for religious duties)
detention:	the action of keeping someone in official custody; keeping one in school after hours
dictate:	to lay down authoritatively; to say or read aloud
animation:	a state of being lively and full of energy; creating a live movement out of successive drawings of things or out of puppets
coalesce:	to come together and form a mass or a whole

Now try to fill in the table below by finding the appropriate root(s) and interpreting the meaning of each word:

Word	Root(s)	Guessed Meaning	Actual Meaning
predict			
retentive			
maneuver			
reclusive			
fluorescent			
animal			
claustrophobia			
amanuensis			
tenable			
conclude			

Lesson 41

THE EX-SPOUSES

Anton knew that he was **culpable** for the great **distress** his wife experienced before their divorce. He had shamelessly cheated on her multiple times. And yet, whenever he spoke with her, Anton could not **simulate** guilt or a feeling of compassion. He felt that she had stolen the best years of his life by refusing to sign the divorce papers much earlier. Anton would **trade** all the money he had in the bank for the chance to get those years back. He knew that his wife only agreed to the divorce when she was convinced that it would **aggrandize** her own wealth, and he did not feel sorry for her.

NEW WORDS

culpable
ˈkəlpəbəl

simulate
ˈsimyəˌlāt

distress
disˈtres

trade
trād

aggrandize
əˈgranˌdīz

Definitions: Try matching the words in the list with the appropriate definitions. If you are stuck, check the glossary in the back of the book or the passage at the top of the page.

1.	culpable	__________	a.	to imitate the appearance or character of
2.	simulate	__________	b.	1. extreme anxiety, sorrow, or pain; 2. troubles caused by lacking money or basic life necessities; (v.) to cause somebody anxiety, sorrow, or pain
3.	distress	__________	c.	worthy of blame
4.	trade	__________	d.	(n.) 1. the action of buying and selling goods and services; 2. a job typically requiring manual skills and specialization; (v.) 1. to buy and sell goods and services; 2. to exchange something for something else, typically as a commercial transaction
5.	aggrandize	__________	e.	to increase the power, status, or wealth of

Sentences: Try to use the words above in a sentence below. Remember that a word ending may be changed or its figure of speech slightly altered.

6. Often indigenous peoples would ____________________ their wares at a local bazaar.
7. These glasses that deliberately blur vision ____________________ the visual consequences of drinking a dozen cans of beer.
8. Jana was in ____________________ when she realized that the plane she was flying was experiencing an engine failure.
9. The Spanish monarchy tried to ____________________ its image by building fancy new castles in the hills.
10. When the jury saw a video of the defendant robbing a bank, they were convinced that he was ____________________ of the crime.

NEW WORDS

craft
kraft

annul
əˈnəl

intercept
ˌintərˈsept

restitution
ˌrestəˈt(y)o͞oSHən

succumb
səˈkəm

Lesson 42

A COURT CASE

The husband Mr. Pfeiffer pleaded with the judge to **annul** the marriage. Mr. Pfeiffer had been able to **intercept** his wife's mail and had many letters from her lover as evidence. In addition, he used his **craft** of persuasion to convince the judge that his wife had to pay him a large sum of money in **restitution** for his damaged reputation. The wife knew that Mr. Pfeiffer was largely exaggerating the situation; however, Mr. Pfeiffer had the judge's full support so she had to **succumb** and agree to pay him the money.

Definitions: Try matching the words in the list with the appropriate definitions. If you are stuck, check the glossary in the back of the book or the passage at the top of the page.

1. craft __________ a. (n.) an activity involving skill and often making things by hand; (v.) to exercise skill in making or doing something
2. annul __________ b. (n.) an act or instance of obstructing someone or something so as to prevent it from continuing to a destination; (v.) to obstruct someone or something so as to prevent it from continuing to a destination
3. intercept __________ c. to declare an official agreement, decision, or result invalid
4. restitution __________ d. 1. the act of returning something lost or stolen to its proper owner; 2. recompense for loss or injury; 3. the restoration of something to its original state
5. succumb __________ e. to fail to resist (pressure, temptation, or some other force)

Sentences: Try to use the words above in a sentence below. Remember that a word ending may be changed or its figure of speech slightly altered.

6. Earl sought ____________________ after his cousin borrowed his flat screen television and refused to return it.
7. The hamlet finally ____________________ to defeat after weeks of barbarian attacks.
8. The basketball player ____________________ the ball, ran to the other end of the court, and made a three-point shot.
9. Artisans can spend years of their lives apprenticed to a master in order to learn a particular ____________________.
10. Charlotte tried to have her marriage to Zack ____________________ because she realized hours after the wedding that the marriage was a huge mistake.

Lesson 43

THROUGH THE GRAPEVINE

Soon after his retirement, Harry decided to establish his **domicile** in the valley, where he purchased a strip of land to create a small vineyard. Some of the locals were quick to warn Harry about the climate being **arid**, insisting that nothing green would grow there for too long. Fortunately, Harry held fast to his expert horticultural knowledge and wine **culture** in particular. When his neighbor made an **arrogant** remark that only a naïve hillbilly would bother trying to harvest anything of value from that land, Harry was heard to simply **retort**: "Just you watch."

NEW WORDS

domicile
ˈdäməˌsīl, ˈdō-, ˈdäməsəl

arid
ˈarid

culture
ˈkəlCHər

retort
riˈtôrt

arrogant
ˈarəgənt

Definitions: Try matching the words in the list with the appropriate definitions. If you are stuck, check the glossary in the back of the book or the passage at the top of the page.

1.	domicile	__________	a.	having or revealing an exaggerated sense of oneself or one's abilities
2.	arid	__________	b.	the arts and other manifestations of human intellectual achievement regarded collectively
3.	culture	__________	c.	the country that a person treats as his or her permanent home
4.	retort	__________	d.	(n.) a sharp, angry, or wittily incisive response to a remark; (v.) to respond to a remark or accusation in a witty or incisive manner
5.	arrogant	__________	e.	land and climate that is dry and barren that is hardly capable of supporting vegetation

Sentences: Try to use the words above in a sentence below. Remember that a word ending may be changed or its figure of speech slightly altered.

6. After two decades of use and deterioration, Armand hired a builder to update and renovate his ____________________.
7. Deserts are noted to be ____________________ places; by definition they lack water that is essential for making many forms of vegetation flourish.
8. Because of the strong influence of Chinese ____________________, many East Asian and Southeast Asian Nations celebrate Lunar New Year.
9. When William accused Lyndon of stealing his briefcase, the latter ____________________ that William was crazy to make such an assertion.
10. Often a(n) ____________________ person will not earn many friends by constantly boasting of his or her talents.

NEW WORDS

benevolent
bəˈnevələnt

encounter
enˈkoun(t)ər

wary
ˈwe(ə)rē

berate
biˈrāt

demonstrate
ˈdemənˌstrāt

Lesson 44

THE CONSERVATIVE FATHER

During their brief **encounter** in the café, the handsome stranger seemed friendly and **benevolent**, and the young girl was charmed by his manners. Yet, she remained **wary** about disclosing too much personal information. She did not overtly **demonstrate** any interest in him. She was well aware that her father – the café owner – was carefully watching her. The old man was very conservative and he would **berate** her every time she even glanced at a man.

Definitions: Try matching the words in the list with the appropriate definitions. If you are stuck, check the glossary in the back of the book or the passage at the top of the page.

1.	benevolent	__________	a.	to scold or criticize someone angrily
2.	encounter	__________	b.	(n.) an unexpected or casual meeting with someone or something; (v.) 1. to unexpectedly experience or be faced with something difficult or hostile; 2. to meet
3.	wary	__________	c.	well-meaning and kindly
4.	berate	__________	d.	feeling or showing caution about possible dangers or problems
5.	demonstrate	__________	e.	1. to clearly show the existence or truth of something by giving proof or evidence; 2. to take part in a public meeting or protest expressing views on a political issue

Sentences: Try to use the words above in a sentence below. Remember that a word ending may be changed or its figure of speech slightly altered.

6. When Kelsey ____________________ her ex-boyfriend in the grocery store, the two coldly stared at each other before continuing with their shopping.
7. It is important to be ____________________ when a former foe tries to be kind to you.
8. The ____________________ old lady baked a batch of cookies for her neighbors.
9. It is easy to ____________________ if you are unhappy about a situation; it is much harder to take action and create a political change.
10. Lynn's parents ____________________ her for staying out past bedtime and partying with her friends.

Lesson 45

THE GULLIBLE TOURISTS

The Nepalese company offered what seemed to be an incredible deal: to **trek** across a famous Himalayan path with an experienced guide at almost no cost. On this trip, the guide spoke to the tourists with **ardor** about the beauty of the mountain trail. The tourists listened with **dutiful** attention to the mountain expert. They had no experience and they were **credulous** enough to trust him completely, even though he had shown them no identification of being a professional guide. They did not know that if they had only looked him up on the Internet, they would have found many negative reviews that would **undermine** his authority.

NEW WORDS

dutiful
ˈd(y)o͞otəfəl

undermine
ˌəndərˈmīn, ˈəndərˌmīn

credulous
ˈkrejələs

trek
trek

ardor
ˈärdər

Definitions: Try matching the words in the list with the appropriate definitions. If you are stuck, check the glossary in the back of the book or the passage at the top of the page.

1.	dutiful	________	a.	exhibiting too great a readiness to believe things
2.	undermine	________	b.	a long arduous journey, especially one made on foot
3.	credulous	________	c.	to damage or weaken something (often an intellectual argument)
4.	trek	________	d.	conscientiously or obediently fulfilling one's role
5.	ardor	________	e.	enthusiasm or passion

Sentences: Try to use the words above in a sentence below. Remember that a word ending may be changed or its figure of speech slightly altered.

6. New evidence ____________________ the research in last year's report, thus making its conclusions increasingly questionable.
7. Lorraine speaks with such ____________________ when she discusses piano teaching.
8. Martin was a(n) ____________________ child and helped his aging parents out with their medical bills.
9. My ____________________ cousin actually believed that America's first president, George Washington (1732-99) is coming over to take him to lunch today.
10. My boy scouts pack went hiking last weekend and ____________________ fifteen miles through the forest.

NEW WORDS

sate
sāt

congenial
kənˈjēnyəl

crisis
ˈkrīsis

prosperous
ˈpräspərəs

nucleus
ˈn(y)o͞oklēəs

Lesson 46

FAMILY HAS YOUR BACK

Eli's family was the **nucleus** of his emotional support. For it was the people closest to him who would always help him during a time of **crisis**. In **prosperous** times and in poor times they all stuck together. The atmosphere in the house was friendly and **congenial**. Whenever things went wrong, Eli went back to the family. This was his way to **sate** his need for comfort and emotional support.

Definitions: Try matching the words in the list with the appropriate definitions. If you are stuck, check the glossary in the back of the book or the passage at the top of the page.

1. sate ________ a. a period of intense difficulty, danger, or trouble
2. congenial ________ b. 1. (of a person) pleasant because of a personality, interests, or other qualities similar to one's own; 2. (of a thing) pleasant or suitable because it is suited to one's tastes or inclination
3. crisis ________ c. flourishing financially; successful in material terms
4. prosperous ________ d. the central and most important part of an object, group, or movement, forming a basis for its development and growth
5. nucleus ________ e. to fully satisfy a desire or appetite

Sentences: Try to use the words above in a sentence below. Remember that a word ending may be changed or its figure of speech slightly altered.

6. In the eyes of many, the ________________ of activity in the United States is New York City.
7. When the town was cut off from its water supply, a(n) ________________ emerged as citizens could neither drink nor bathe.
8. Nothing could ________________ the child's appetite: he kept eating endlessly as if there were no end in sight.
9. Hard work and a good education can truly help people to have ________________ lives.
10. A sales person ought to be ________________, for a negative attitude can really put off customers.

Lesson 47

NOT IN MY BACK YARD

The new neighborhood policy will **oblige** the residents of Atwood Circle to pursue a solution concerning the **flux** of **pungent** waters flowing downstream from their homes. It will become forbidden to release liquid detergents that circulate in the communal waters. **Strenuous** efforts already have been made by community firefighters to neutralize the contamination. The **dogged** firefighters declared that there should be a severe fine for anyone found polluting the communal waters in the future.

NEW WORDS

oblige
ə'blīj

flux
fləks

strenuous
'strenyo͞oəs

pungent
'pənjənt

dogged
'dôgid

Definitions: Try matching the words in the list with the appropriate definitions. If you are stuck, check the glossary in the back of the book or the passage at the top of the page.

1.	oblige	________	a.	1. the action or process of flowing or flowing out; 2. continuous change
2.	flux	________	b.	requiring or using great exertion
3.	strenuous	________	c.	to make someone morally or legally bound to an action or course of action
4.	pungent	________	d.	having a sharply strong smell or taste
5.	dogged	________	e.	having or showing tenacity and grim persistence

Sentences: Try to use the words above in a sentence below. Remember that a word ending may be changed or its figure of speech slightly altered.

6. Running a marathon is ____________________ work; it requires a lot of training and exertion for hours on end.
7. Shad sat on his rooftop and watched the ____________________ of people entering and exiting the stadium all day long.
8. The incense burning in the living room has a(n) ____________________ smell.
9. Even though it was clear that Brian was not going to win the triathlon, his ____________________ determination prevented him from giving up.
10. Francis felt ____________________ to attend the dinner banquet since three of his students were winning awards at the event.

NEW WORDS

basis
ˈbāsis

inspect
inˈspekt

prolong
prəˈlôNG, -ˈläNG

blueprint
ˈblo͞oˌprint

fluctuate
ˈfləkCHo͞oˌāt

Lesson 48

MAKING A DREAM COME TRUE

Angel created a detailed **blueprint** for becoming a top-tier chef in the upcoming five years. She knew she could achieve her goal on the **basis** of her good education and exemplary work experience. Angel was aware that success could **fluctuate** and that she had to be prepared for some challenges. For example, even though her boss told her that she would be ready to become a sous-chef in one year, he could also **prolong** her training if he deemed that necessary. Angel knew that her boss liked to **inspect** every single detail of her work; therefore, she took extra care on every little detail.

Definitions: Try matching the words in the list with the appropriate definitions. If you are stuck, check the glossary in the back of the book or the passage at the top of the page.

1. basis __________ a. the underlying support or foundation for an idea, argument, or process
2. inspect __________ b. to rise and fall irregularly in number or amount
3. prolong __________ c. a design plan or technical drawing (used heavily in architecture); something that acts as a plan, model, or template
4. blueprint __________ d. to examine someone or something closely to assess condition and/or shortcomings
5. fluctuate __________ e. to extend the duration of

Sentences: Try to use the words above in a sentence below. Remember that a word ending may be changed or its figure of speech slightly altered.

6. The architect revealed a(n) ____________________ of the new skyscraper at this morning's design conference.
7. It is normal for the temperature to ____________________ throughout the day.
8. The professor was able to ____________________ his speech by elaborating in detail on three of his slides.
9. It is important to ____________________ a home before purchasing it to ensure that there are no major problems.
10. The treasurer used previous years' expense totals as the ____________________ for his financial assessment for this year's projected expenses.

Lesson 49

A CAMPUS TORN BY WAR

The student magazine was renowned for its **pacifist** stance on the ongoing war. It was thus no surprise when the magazine fell **prey** to the rising hawkish sentiments on campus. Someone set fire to the publication's office and it suffered **severe** damage as a result. The campus community did **deplore** the blatant attack; however, no one was charged for the crime. After much investigation, the campus police finally found some **authentic** evidence that pointed at the possible perpetrators. They were part of a secret campus group that was funded by one of the warring parties.

NEW WORDS

severe
səˈvi(ə)r

prey
prā

pacifist
ˈpasəˌfist

authentic
ôˈTHentik

deplore
diˈplôr

Definitions: Try matching the words in the list with the appropriate definitions. If you are stuck, check the glossary in the back of the book or the passage at the top of the page.

1. severe __________ a. genuine, of undisputed origin; based on facts, accurate, reliable
2. prey __________ b. to feel or express strong disapproval of (something)
3. pacifist __________ c. (n.) 1. an animal that is hunted or killed by another for food; 2. a person easily injured or taken advantage of; (v.) 1. to hunt and kill for food; 2. to take advantage of
4. authentic __________ d. one who believes war and violence are unjustifiable
5. deplore __________ e. very great or intense; very strict or harsh

Sentences: Try to use the words above in a sentence below. Remember that a word ending may be changed or its figure of speech slightly altered.

6. As a(n) ____________________, Trey has decided never to fight or to advocate war as long as he lives.
7. While a minor cut is not a serious injury, being paralyzed below the waist is a(n) ____________________ injury.
8. Foxes tend to view rabbits as their ____________________: the latter are hunted as a food source.
9. Even though Shirley is not Japanese, her miso soup tastes really ____________________.
10. Though most of Anya's teachers ____________________ her, none can object to the quality of her excellent academic work.

NEW WORDS

muster
ˈməstər

acquaintance
əˈkwāntns

covert
ˈkōvərt, kōˈvərt, ˈkəvərt

voluminous
vəˈlo͞omənəs

initiate
iˈniSHēˌāt

Lesson 50

THE LOVE LETTER

Janet was Phil's **acquaintance** whom he had met through mutual friends on a few occasions. Phil had a **covert** interest in Janet; however, he could not **muster** the courage to call her on the phone and ask her out on a date. It was not easy for him to **initiate** conversations with attractive girls because he was too self-aware of his speech impediment. Instead, he wrote Janet a **voluminous** letter, in which he poured out his feelings for her.

Definitions: Try matching the words in the list with the appropriate definitions. If you are stuck, check the glossary in the back of the book or the passage at the top of the page.

1.	muster	__________	a.	1. to cause something to begin; 2. to admit someone into a secret society or group
2.	acquaintance	__________	b.	not openly acknowledged or displayed
3.	covert	__________	c.	occupying much space
4.	voluminous	__________	d.	1. a person's knowledge or experience of something; 2. a person one knows slightly but who is not a close friend
5.	initiate	__________	e.	to summon up a feeling, attitude, or response

Sentences: Try to use the words above in a sentence below. Remember that a word ending may be changed or its figure of speech slightly altered.

6. The man in the grey suit is my ____________________ from college.
7. It was difficult to ____________________ a conversation with the broker because his telephone was broken.
8. It took weeks for the new employee to ____________________ enough courage to ask his boss for a raise.
9. That artwork is ____________________ and cannot even fit on the available wall space.
10. Most times people who try to cheat others in business are ____________________ in their operation.

Crossword Puzzle

Lessons 41-50

ACROSS

2 (adj.) very great or intense; very strict or harsh
6 (adj.) having a sharply strong smell or taste
7 (v.) 1. to cause something to begin; 2. to admit someone into a secret society or group
8 (n.) 1. the act of returning something lost or stolen to its proper owner; 2. recompense for loss or injury; 3. the restoration of something to its original state
9 (n.) a long arduous journey, especially one made on foot
10 (adj.) 1. (of a person) pleasant because of a personality, interests, or other qualities similar to one's own; 2. (of a thing) pleasant or suitable because it is suited to one's tastes or inclination
11 (v.) to examine someone or something closely to assess condition and/or shortcomings
12 (n.) the underlying support or foundation for an idea, argument, or process
16 (n.) a sharp, angry, or wittily incisive response to a remark; (v.) to respond to a remark or accusation in a witty or incisive manner
17 (adj.) genuine, of undisputed origin; based on facts, accurate, reliable
18 (adj.) conscientiously or obediently fulfilling one's role
19 (n.) the arts and other manifestations of human intellectual achievement regarded collectively

DOWN

1 (v.) to scold or criticize someone angrily
2 (v.) to fully satisfy a desire or appetite
3 (v.) to summon up a feeling, attitude, or response
4 (v.) to increase the power, status, or wealth of
5 (n.) an unexpected or casual meeting with someone or something; (v.) 1. to unexpectedly experience or be faced with something difficult or hostile; 2. to meet
13 (v.) to imitate the appearance or character of
14 (v.) to fail to resist (pressure, temptation, or some other force)
15 (v.) to make someone morally or legally bound to an action or course of action

Vocabulary Review
Lessons 41-50

Directions: Match each word with its best approximate definition. Note that definitions are not necessarily repeated verbatim from the lesson exercises.

	Word			Definition
1.	culpable	________	a.	passion or enthusiasm
2.	distress	________	b.	to extend the duration of
3.	craft	________	c.	well meaning and kindly
4.	annul	________	d.	requiring or using great exertion
5.	domicile	________	e.	one who believes that war and violence are unjustifiable
6.	arid	________	f.	a person's home or residence, or the country in which a person considers his or her home or residence
7.	benevolent	________	g.	a period of trouble, difficulty, or danger
8.	wary	________	h.	to declare an agreement, decision, or result invalid; to declare a marriage to have no legal existence
9.	credulous	________	i.	having little to no rain; too dry for vegetation to grow
10.	ardor	________	j.	exhibiting tenacity and grim persistence
11.	crisis	________	k.	to rise and fall regularly in number or amount
12.	prosperous	________	l.	worthy of blame
13.	strenuous	________	m.	successful in material terms; flourishing financially
14.	dogged	________	n.	extreme anxiety or pain, or to cause someone such
15.	prolong	________	o.	not openly acknowledged or displayed
16.	fluctuate	________	p.	having or showing too great a readiness to believe things
17.	pacifist	________	q.	an activity where one makes things by hand
18.	deplore	________	r.	occupying much space
19.	covert	________	s.	to feel strong disapproval of something
20.	voluminous	________	t.	exhibiting caution about possible dangers or problems

Word Roots: Unit 5

ROOTS AND THEIR MEANINGS

dis:	**apart, away from, not**	**pun/pen:**	**to pay, punish, compensate**
nom/nym:	**name**	**us/ut:**	**to use**
gno:	**to know**	**un/non:**	**not**

Here are a few examples of some words that use the above roots:

disengaged: emotionally unattached
homonym: two or more words having the same spelling but different meanings
agnostic: a person who claims neither faith nor nonbelief in God
punitive: inflicting or intended to be punishment; a charge or tax that is exorbitantly high
utensil: an implement for household usage
uninspired: lacking in imagination, commitment, or originality
noncommittal: not willing to stick to a definite course of action

Now try to fill in the table below by finding the appropriate root(s) and interpreting the meaning of each word:

Word	Root(s)	Guessed Meaning	Actual Meaning
nomenclature			
penalty			
diagnostic			
unintelligent			
disrespectful			
reusable			
ignorant			
nonessential			
pseudonym			

Specific Vocabularies I

Measurement, Music, and Instrument Words

Some Measurement Equivalents:

Length Equivalents

- 12 inches = 1 foot
- 3 feet = 1 yard
- 5,280 feet = 1 mile
- 1 ton = 2,000 pounds
- 1 fathom = 6 feet (typically used to measure depth in water)

Time Equivalents

- Approximately 52 weeks = 1 year
- 1 fortnight = 2 weeks

Liquid and Powder Equivalents

- 2 pints = 1 quart
- 4 quarts = 1 gallon
- 3 teaspoons = 1 tablespoon

Some Measurement Equivalents:

- **Decibels** measures the intensity of sound
- **Lumens** measure the intensity of light
- **Watts** are a measure of power in an electric circuit
- **Volts** measure the amount of electrical potential in something
- **Amperes** measure the flow of an electric current
- **Flux** measures the amount of electric or magnetic field passing through an area

Some Music Terms:

- A singer with a low voice is called a **bass**
- A singer with a high voice is called a **tenor**
- The speed at which a passage of music should be played is called the **tempo**
- A written representation of a musical composition showing all the vocal and instrumental parts arranged is called a **score**
- Wind instruments that are made of metal are called **brass** instruments; they include trumpets, saxophones, horns, tuba, and trombone
- Wind instruments not made of brass are called **woodwind**; examples include clarinets, flutes, oboes, and bassoons.

- Instruments where one strikes an object to produce sound are called **percussion** instruments; examples include drums, bells, xylophones, cymbals, gongs, and rattles
- A **conductor** is a person who directs the performance of an orchestra or choir

Some Instrument Terms:

- A **thermometer** measures temperature
- A **barometer** measures atmospheric pressure
- A **hygrometer** measures the humidity of the air or a gas
- A **metronome** is a device that marks (musical) time at a selected rate by giving a regular tick
- An **awl** is a small pointed tool for piercing holes, especially in leather
- One uses **pliers** to grip small objects or to bend wire
- A **jack** is a device to lift heavy objects, especially cars, so that wheels can be changed
- A **protractor** is a device used to measure angles
- There are two instruments called a **compass**; one helps find direction relative to magnetic north and the other is used to draw circles, to draw arcs, and to measure distances between points
- A **stethoscope** is an instrument used by a doctor to listen to one's breathing and heartbeat

NEW WORDS

universal
ˌyo͞onəˈvərsəl

adorn
əˈdôrn

mute
myo͞ot

adversity
adˈvərsitē

marvel
ˈmärvəl

Lesson 51

THE POWER OF ART

The captured painter, who had now become a slave to the Sultan, showed great courage in the face of **adversity**. He humbly asked for some paint and created a large painting for his captor. When the Sultan's attendants saw the painting, there was **mute** admiration in their eyes. They didn't dare say a word but one could clearly see the look of **marvel** in their faces. The painting expressed some **universal** feelings, such as sadness and nostalgia, and the attendants could relate to them. The Sultan himself was so impressed that he decided to **adorn** the walls of his palace with the captured painter's work.

Definitions: Try matching the words in the list with the appropriate definitions. If you are stuck, check the glossary in the back of the book or the passage at the top of the page.

1.	universal	________	a.	of or done by all people
2.	adorn	________	b.	(n.) an astonishing or wonderful person or thing; (v.) to be filled with wonder or astonishment
3.	mute	________	c.	(adj.) refraining from speech or temporarily speechless; (n.) a person without the power of speech; (v.) to deaden, muffle, or soften the sound of
4.	adversity	________	d.	difficulty or misfortune
5.	marvel	________	e.	to make more beautiful or attractive

Sentences: Try to use the words above in a sentence below. Remember that a word ending may be changed or its figure of speech slightly altered.

6. Elvis put the television on ____________________ so that he could concentrate on his math homework.
7. Though the world contains many cultures, it is ____________________ true that cannibalism is frowned upon.
8. Often individuals who have persevered in the face of ____________________ are kinder than those who have not.
9. Mikayla helped ____________________ the tree with lights and ornaments.
10. I could not help but to ____________________ at the magician's amazing illusions.

Lesson 52

THE PROFESSOR'S TIME AWAY

Ever since the professor went on **sabbatical** after seven years of incessant work, his wife could perceive a clear change in his behavior. The professor picked up some **eccentric** habits, such as sitting outside in the yard early in the morning mumbling with a cup of rum and tea. After drinking his alcoholic **beverage**, the professor would get somewhat **unruly** and run through the house, occasionally breaking something. His wife could not comprehend this **irrational** behavior, especially since her husband had always been a very sensible person. When she broached the subject, he just said that he needed to let off some steam.

NEW WORDS

irrational
iˈraSHənl

beverage
ˈbev(ə)rij

sabbatical
səˈbatikəl

eccentric
ikˈsentrik

unruly
ˌənˈro͞olē

Definitions: Try matching the words in the list with the appropriate definitions. If you are stuck, check the glossary in the back of the book or the passage at the top of the page.

1.	irrational	__________	a.	not logical or reasonable
2.	beverage	__________	b.	(adj.) 1. unconventional and slightly strange; 2. off-center (n.) a person with unconventional and slightly strange behavior
3.	sabbatical	__________	c.	a period of paid leave granted for study or travel
4.	eccentric	__________	d.	a drink
5.	unruly	__________	e.	disorderly, disruptive, and not amenable to discipline or control

Sentences: Try to use the words above in a sentence below. Remember that a word ending may be changed or its figure of speech slightly altered.

6. It is ____________________ to think that if you spend all of your money, more will suddenly appear.
7. Molly is a(n) ____________________ person because she often mumbles and her house is filled with wacky science experiments; nevertheless, she is very kind.
8. The lunch special includes a burger, fries, dessert, and your choice of ____________________ to drink.
9. Most professors receive a(n) ____________________ every seventh year to pursue research interests.
10. The ____________________ child kept jumping around and faked crying during lessons to avoid work.

Lesson 53

NEW WORDS

alleviate
əˈlēvēˌāt

amalgamation
əˈmalgəˌmāt

feat
fēt

vulnerable
ˈvəln(ə)rəbəl

gesture
ˈjesCHər

CHANGING TIMES

The **amalgamation** of the two companies created a lot of tension among the employees. To **alleviate** the pressure among them, the new CEO invested much time in team building and giving personal attention to each of the workers. That proved to be a very thoughtful **gesture** on his part that seemed to produce good results. Getting all the employees to work together as a team was no small **feat**, considering how different the two companies were from each other before the merger. It was a **vulnerable** time for the new company, but the CEO felt confident that things would get much better with time and that the company would soon become one of the main competitors in the market.

Definitions: Try matching the words in the list with the appropriate definitions. If you are stuck, check the glossary in the back of the book or the passage at the top of the page.

1.	alleviate	________	a.	to make pain or suffering less severe
2.	amalgamation	________	b.	(n.) a movement of the body, especially the hand or head, to express an idea or meaning, or to convey one's feelings or intentions; (v.) to move a part of the body, especially the hand or head, to express an idea or m meaning, or to convey one's feelings or intentions
3.	feat	________	c.	an action or achievement that requires great courage or skill
4.	vulnerable	________	d.	the action, process, or result of uniting or combining
5.	gesture	________	e.	susceptible to physical or emotional harm

Sentences: Try to use the words above in a sentence below. Remember that a word ending may be changed or its figure of speech slightly altered.

6. The jar in the kitchen contains a(n) ____________________ of different sweets.
7. It was a difficult ____________________ for the acrobat to jump through three flaming hoops and land on her feet.
8. One is ____________________ to attack if he or she goes into the area beyond the hill that is not protected by the military.
9. I took three pills to help ____________________ my headache.
10. Amos made a(n) ____________________ with his hands to tell us that we should follow him to the park.

Lesson 54

THE DIFFERENCE BETWEEN WORDS AND REALITY

The crowd was **jubilant**. Its candidate had just won the local **election**. However, after the election it slowly became evident that there was a **fissure** between the politician's promises and his actions. When he gave a **synopsis** of his policies after his first three months of office, his supporters were disappointed. The politician had dabbled in **miscellaneous** issues; however, he did not seem to have made true on any of his promises.

NEW WORDS

jubilant
ˈjo͞obələnt

election
iˈlekSHən

miscellaneous
ˌmisəˈlānēəs

fissure
ˈfiSHər

synopsis
səˈnäpsis

Definitions: Try matching the words in the list with the appropriate definitions. If you are stuck, check the glossary in the back of the book or the passage at the top of the page.

1. jubilant __________
2. election __________
3. miscellaneous ________
4. fissure __________
5. synopsis __________

a. a brief summary or general survey of something
b. (of items or people) of various types or from different sources
c. (n.) a long narrow opening made by cracking or splitting, especially in the earth; (v.) to split or crack something to cause a long narrow opening
d. feeling or expressing great happiness
e. a formal organized process of selecting or being selected, typically for members of a political party

Sentences: Try to use the words above in a sentence below. Remember that a word ending may be changed or its figure of speech slightly altered.

6. One can see a(n) ____________________ in the earth where the fault line runs.
7. Anita was ____________________ when she heard that she would be head counselor at the school.
8. Every four years the United States holds a(n) ____________________ where people vote for their choice of president.
9. Ross left ____________________ toys strewn all over the floor of the living room.
10. A(n) ____________________ of the book can be found on its back cover.

NEW WORDS

mandatory
'mandə,terē

authoritarian
ə,THôri'te(ə)rēən, ô,THär-

ailment
'ālmənt

deluge
'del(y)o͞oj

underlying
,əndər'lī-iNG

Lesson 55

STRESS DURING CHRISTMAS

Just before Christmas, Sandy received a **deluge** of letters to proofread at work. She had an ongoing **ailment** for about two weeks and wanted to postpone the work until after New Year's. However, she knew that her **authoritarian** boss would not give her the days off. For him, work was **mandatory** unless one had a really serious condition that required hospitalization. She was not aware that the **underlying** cause for her boss' harsh behavior was his fear that the company might go bankrupt after a year of sluggish business.

Definitions: Try matching the words in the list with the appropriate definitions. If you are stuck, check the glossary in the back of the book or the passage at the top of the page.

1.	mandatory ________	a.	to be the cause or basis of
2.	authoritarian ________	b.	required by law or rules; compulsory
3.	ailment ________	c.	(n.) a severe flood; (v.) to flood or be flooded by a great quantity of something
4.	deluge ________	d.	an illness (typically minor illness)
5.	underlying ________	e.	favoring or enforcing strict obedience to authority, especially the government at the expense of personal freedom; showing a lack of concern about the wishes or cares of others

Sentences: Try to use the words above in a sentence below. Remember that a word ending may be changed or its figure of speech slightly altered.

6. Many people found the adolescent's ____________________ behavior to be a major turn-off.
7. It is ____________________ that all employees attend tonight's meeting; if they do not attend, their positions may be terminated.
8. Good medicine should help cure your ____________________.
9. Ginny was ____________________ with homework after she received research assignments in all of her seven classes.
10. While pundits say charisma is important for getting elected, the ____________________ factor swinging election outcomes is usually economic health.

Lesson 56

DIFFERENT GENERATIONS

After inheriting the company from his father, Misha decided to **rejuvenate** the business. He made a **spontaneous** decision to **transact** with a number of foreign companies – something his conservative father had avoided. Unlike his father, Misha was a **gregarious** young man who wanted to open up the company to as many new markets as possible. He also did not care so much for his father's aristocratic clients. In fact, Misha hired some new employees from a **humble** background who could help him transform the company's services in order to be more accessible to regular customers. The old aristocratic days of the company were over.

NEW WORDS

spontaneous
spän'tānēəs

rejuvenate
ri'jo͞ovəˌnāt

humble
'həmbəl

transact
tran'sakt, -'zakt

gregarious
gri'ge(ə)rēəs

Definitions: Try matching the words in the list with the appropriate definitions. If you are stuck, check the glossary in the back of the book or the passage at the top of the page.

1.	spontaneous ________	a.	to make someone or something feel fresher or younger
2.	rejuvenate ________	b.	a person who is fond of company, sociable
3.	humble ________	c.	to conduct or carry out (business)
4.	transact ________	d.	(n.) 1. having or showing a modest or low estimate of one's importance; 2. of low social, administrative, or political rank; (v.) to lower (someone) in dignity or importance
5.	gregarious ________	e.	performed by impulse and without any planning or premeditation

Sentences: Try to use the words above in a sentence below. Remember that a word ending may be changed or its figure of speech slightly altered.

6. Mitt's decision to go on a vacation to El Paso was ____________________: without any planning he bought a ticket and was on a plane only five hours later.
7. Hot springs are noted for their ability to ____________________ people who are exhausted and need an extra boost of energy.
8. It is difficult to ____________________ business with people from two completely different cultures.
9. Because Zoe is a(n) ____________________ person, she finds great joy in going to social events with her friends.
10. Casey was ____________________ when she received the award: rather than discussing herself, she thanked all of the people who helped her along the way.

NEW WORDS

transparent
tran'spe(ə)rənt, -'spar-

timorous
'timərəs

incite
in'sīt

cavort
kə'vôrt

triumph
'trīəmf

Lesson 57

THE SHY STUDENT

While most of the children would **cavort** in the yard each afternoon, the **timorous** little boy stood aloof and just looked at them. It was **transparent** that he was too shy to participate. In order to **incite** the boy to play, his schoolteacher asked some of the other boys to approach him and throw a ball towards him. She was determined to help the timid student. She knew that if he could overcome his shyness it would be a professional **triumph** for her.

Definitions: Try matching the words in the list with the appropriate definitions. If you are stuck, check the glossary in the back of the book or the passage at the top of the page.

1.	transparent ________		a.	to encourage or stir up (violent or unlawful behavior)
2.	timorous ________		b.	a great victory or achievement
3.	incite ________		c.	1. allowing light to pass through so that objects are easily seen; 2. easy to perceive or detect; having thoughts or feelings that are easy to detect
4.	cavort ________		d.	to jump or dance around excitedly
5.	triumph ________		e.	showing or suffering from nervousness, fear, or lack of confidence

Sentences: Try to use the words above in a sentence below. Remember that a word ending may be changed or its figure of speech slightly altered.

6. After four months of battle, the rebel forces finally were able to ____________________ and win the war.
7. The ____________________ sailor felt anxiety confronting his volatile captain about the squalid condition of the galley.
8. It became ____________________ that Joel did not do his homework when he was unable to give an impromptu oral presentation on the subject.
9. Often at tribal ceremonies, adolescents will ____________________ around before a ceremonial fire.
10. Protestors last night ____________________ a fight after one of them hurled a rock at an inattentive police officer.

Lesson 58

THE FIRST STEP

Growing up in a home that was **rife** with tension and abuse, Krysta became a **timid** child who never dared to **vex** her parents with any demands. There was even an unspoken **custom** in her household that Krysta needed to hand over to her alcoholic parents all that she earned from her part-time job. However, when her friends kept boasting of their summer excursions, Krysta was unable to **quench** her thirst for traveling. To afford the European vacation that she wanted so badly, Krysta secretly saved up money behind her parents' backs.

NEW WORDS

custom
ˈkəstəm

vex
veks

quench
kwenCH

timid
ˈtimid

rife
rīf

Definitions: Try matching the words in the list with the appropriate definitions. If you are stuck, check the glossary in the back of the book or the passage at the top of the page.

1.	custom	__________	a.	(especially of something undesirable or harmful) of common occurrence; widespread
2.	vex	__________	b.	(adj.) made or done for a particular customer; (n.) a traditional and widely accepted way of behaving or doing something that is specific to a particular society, place, or time
3.	quench	__________	c.	to make one feel annoyed, frustrated, or worried, especially with trivial matters
4.	timid	__________	d.	to satisfy one's thirst by drinking; to satisfy a desire
5.	rife	__________	e.	showing a lack of courage or confidence; frightened

Sentences: Try to use the words above in a sentence below. Remember that a word ending may be changed or its figure of speech slightly altered.

6. The puerile child continued to ____________________ the guests through the entire dinner party.
7. Those suits were ____________________ made for the tall basketball players.
8. It can take a lot of courage for a(n) ____________________ person to stand up and speak out.
9. Sadly, the woman's story was ____________________ with lies and she could neither be believed nor trusted in the end.
10. Hopefully a glass of lemonade will help ____________________ your thirst.

NEW WORDS

magnitude
ˈmagnəˌtood

mundane
ˌmənˈdān

suspend
səˈspend

verify
ˈverəˌfī

exquisite
ekˈskwizit, ˈekskwizit

Lesson 59

DIVORCE COMPLICATIONS

The divorce was the greatest challenge that Roosevelt had ever faced. The **magnitude** of the event could not be overstated: he was about to lose his family as well as his wife's share in the company. The impending divorce caused him to **suspend** his **mundane** affairs; nothing was as important as trying to repair things with his wife. He took her to some expensive restaurants and treated her with **exquisite** care. Roosevelt wanted to **verify** that, even if they separated, his wife would not cause too much trouble in company affairs.

Definitions: Try matching the words in the list with the appropriate definitions. If you are stuck, check the glossary in the back of the book or the passage at the top of the page.

1.	magnitude	________	a.	extremely beautiful and delicate; intensely felt; highly sensitive or discriminating
2.	mundane	________	b.	1. to temporarily prevent from continuing to be in force or in effect; to defer or delay an action or judgment; 2. to hang something from somewhere
3.	suspend	________	c.	to ensure that something is true, accurate, or justified
4.	verify	________	d.	1. the size or extent of something; 2. size
5.	exquisite	________	e.	lacking excitement or interest; dull

Sentences: Try to use the words above in a sentence below. Remember that a word ending may be changed or its figure of speech slightly altered.

6. A litmus test should help to ____________________ whether the solution is an acid or a base.
7. I wish I could enjoy ____________________ tasks like going grocery shopping, doing crossword puzzles, or cleaning dishes.
8. The crystal chandelier and the beautiful cutlery make the dining room look truly ____________________.
9. Even though the model airplane has hooks to hang it, I am still having difficulty trying to ____________________ it from the ceiling.
10. Vishnu did not realize the ____________________ of the plague until he reached the town and saw thousands of sick citizens.

Lesson 60

THE AMICABLE POLITICIAN

There was something kind about the politician's **physiognomy**. The **focal** point of his face was the look in his eyes: gracious, warm, and magnanimous. His eyes reflected the feeling of **amity** towards everyone. Perhaps that was the reason he was able to **accumulate** so much support from the public in his two **sequential** terms of service. He would have probably won a third term if the law permitted it.

NEW WORDS

physiognomy
ˌfizēˈä(g)nəmē

focal
ˈfōkəl

accumulate
əˈkyo͞omyəˌlāt

sequential
siˈkwenCHəl

amity
ˈamitē

Definitions: Try matching the words in the list with the appropriate definitions. If you are stuck, check the glossary in the back of the book or the passage at the top of the page.

1.	physiognomy ________	a.	a person's facial features or expression, especially when regarded as indicative of character or ethnic origin; the art of judging character from facial characteristics
2.	focal ________	b.	a friendly relationship
3.	accumulate ________	c.	of or relating to the center or main point of interest
4.	sequential ________	d.	forming or following in a logical order
5.	amity ________	e.	to gather together or acquire an increasing number or amount of

Sentences: Try to use the words above in a sentence below. Remember that a word ending may be changed or its figure of speech slightly altered.

6. Because of the ____________________ in our workplace, all employees tend to look out for each other.
7. In the nineteenth century, ____________________ was considered important to some, as one's facial features were thought to explain one's character and motives.
8. The ____________________ point of the presentation was about the widespread problems caused by immigration into the country.
9. Reince took the files from his clients and put them in ____________________ order, indexing them alphabetically by his clients' surnames.
10. Because Lee had not cleaned her room in weeks, the dirty clothes and papers on her floor began to ____________________.

Word Search

Lessons 51-60

```
S U O E N A T N O P S N K Q
U N I V E R S A L F E A T S
A C C U M U L A T E R M U T
Y L B T E K F S I E Q O T V
W M A S T T Y I D L R V U Q
Y Y O N A N A U S O M L Q V
X R P N O B T N M S N E E J
S D O P G I B I E E U X N C
C U S T N O T A R V M R A T
U I S G A T I A T A U V E Q
S Y A P L D B S R I O J L Y
T M R L E L N V Y R C G E Z
O W X V E N E A T H I A W R
M T W J R L D D M M P N L J
```

1 (adj.) of or done by all people
2 (n.) an astonishing or wonderful person or thing; (v.) to be filled with wonder or astonishment
3 (adj.) not logical or reasonable
4 (n.) a period of paid leave granted to for study or travel
5 (n.) an action or achievement that requires great courage or skill
6 (adj.) susceptible to physical or emotional harm
7 (n.) a long narrow opening made by cracking or splitting, especially in the earth; (v.) to split or crack something to cause a long narrow opening
8 (n.) a brief summary or general survey of something
9 (adj.) required by law or rules; compulsory
10 (n.) an illness (typically minor illness)
11 (adj.) performed by impulse and without any planning or premeditation
12 (v.) to make someone or something feel fresher or younger
13 (adj.) showing or suffering from nervousness, fear, or lack of confidence
14 (v.) to jump or dance around excitedly
15 (adj.) made or done for a particular customer; (n.) a traditional and widely accepted way of behaving or doing something that is specific to a particular society, place, or time
16 (v.) to make one feel annoyed, frustrated, or worried, especially with trivial matters
17 (n.) 1. the size or extent of something; 2. size
18 (v.) 1. to temporarily prevent from continuing to be in force or in effect; to defer or delay an action or judgment; 2. to hang something from somewhere
19 (n.) a person's facial features or expression, especially when regarded as indicative of character or ethic origin; the art of judging character from facial characteristics
20 (v.) to gather together or acquire an increasing number or amount of

Vocabulary Review
Lessons 51-60

Directions: Match each word with its best approximate definition. Note that definitions are not necessarily repeated verbatim from the lesson exercises.

1. adorn ________
2. adversity ________
3. beverage ________
4. eccentric ________
5. alleviate ________
6. amalgamation ________
7. jubilant ________
8. election ________
9. deluge ________
10. underlying ________
11. transact ________
12. gregarious ________
13. incite ________
14. triumph ________
15. quench ________
16. timid ________
17. mundane ________
18. verify ________
19. focal ________
20. sequential ________

a. to satisfy one's thirst by drinking
b. of or relating to the center or main point of interest
c. a great victory or achievement; to achieve a great victory
d. a drink, typically not water
e. the action or process of combining or uniting
f. feeling or expressing triumph and joy
g. to make sure and demonstrate that something is true or accurate
h. to conduct or carry out business
i. to be the cause or basis of something
j. to stir up or provoke (violent or unlawful behavior)
k. concerning a person who is unconventional and slightly strange
l. to make pain, a problem, or a deficiency seem less severe
m. a person who is sociable or who enjoys company
n. forming or following in a logical order
o. a process whereby people vote for representatives or to make decisions, typically a political process
p. exhibiting a lack of confidence or courage
q. to make beautiful or attractive
r. lacking excitement; dull
s. a severe flood
t. difficulties or misfortune

Word Roots: Unit 6

ROOTS AND THEIR MEANINGS

spec:	**to look, appear**	**de:**	**away from, opposite of**
gyn:	**woman**	**tact:**	**touch**
sed/sid:	**to sit, be still**	**corp:**	**body**

Here are a few examples of some words that use the above roots:

spectacle: a visually striking performance or play
misogynistic: referring to a hatred of women
sedentary: tending to spend much time seated down; inactive or inert
depart: to leave, often in order to embark on a journey
tactile: of or related to the sense of touch; tangible
corpse: a dead human body

Now try to fill in the table below by finding the appropriate root(s) and interpreting the meaning of each word:

Word	Root(s)	Guessed Meaning	Actual Meaning
deposit			
androgynous			
sediment			
corpus			
speculate			
preside			
contact			
detract			
retrospect			

Lesson 61

IMPASSIVE IRENE

Even though Irene appears to have a stolid demeanor, beneath her inanimate **exterior** she is quite emotive. In fact, when she gets excited about something she can become quite **dynamic** and engaging. Under such conditions, little will **inhibit** her from becoming passionately involved. That said, unless a topic is of more than **incidental** value, Irene will not be too interested. Chances are that you will wind up in a **stalemate** if you spend hours of your time trying to excite her about something that does not move her.

NEW WORDS

incidental
ˌinsiˈdentl

stalemate
ˈstātmənt

dynamic
dīˈnamik

inhibit
inˈhibit

exterior
ikˈsti(ə)rēər

Definitions: Try matching the words in the list with the appropriate definitions. If you are stuck, check the glossary in the back of the book or the passage at the top of the page.

1.	incidental	__________	a.	characterized by constant change, activity, or progress
2.	stalemate	__________	b.	(adj.) forming, existing on, or related to the outside of something; (n.) the outer surface or structure of something
3.	dynamic	__________	c.	to hinder, restrain, or prevent an action or process; to make someone self-conscious and unable to act in a natural way
4.	inhibit	__________	d.	a situation where further action or progress by opposing parties seems impossible; a draw
5.	exterior	__________	e.	accompanying but not a major part of something

Sentences: Try to use the words above in a sentence below. Remember that a word ending may be changed or its figure of speech slightly altered.

6. The ____________________ of the house looked beautiful after its roof had been redone and its windows had been replaced.
7. After three years of fighting, Meredith and Elliot reached a(n) ____________________: neither of them could get what they wanted without losing more in the process.
8. Whether the hotel room has green tea toothpaste is a(n) ____________________ matter compared to whether the quality of room and service is excellent.
9. Felix is a(n) ____________________ character: he is always moving about and doing exciting things.
10. The recent earthquake has ____________________ progress on the construction of the new civic center.

Lesson 62

NEW WORDS

remiss
riˈmis

fatigue
fəˈtēg

supreme
səˈprēm, so͞o-

adamant
ˈadəmənt

harrowing
ˈharōiNG

SOMETHING TO LIVE FOR

The old gardener began to suffer from signs of chronic **fatigue**. He had to stop and rest every fifteen minutes. It seemed to him that each simple action required **supreme** effort. Despite this, the old gardener remained **adamant** about coming to work each morning. He was never **remiss** in his job, regardless of how difficult it had become for him. He knew that the day he retired would be a **harrowing** one: the garden was the old man's whole world in his lonely years as an elderly widower.

Definitions: Try matching the words in the list with the appropriate definitions. If you are stuck, check the glossary in the back of the book or the passage at the top of the page.

1.	remiss	__________	a.	acutely distressing
2.	fatigue	__________	b.	refusing to be persuaded or change one's mind
3.	supreme	__________	c.	superior to all others; strongest, most important, or most powerful; very great or intense
4.	adamant	__________	d.	extreme tiredness, especially resulting from mental or physical exertion or illness
5.	harrowing	__________	e.	lacking care or attention to duty; negligent

Sentences: Try to use the words above in a sentence below. Remember that a word ending may be changed or its figure of speech slightly altered.

6. It would be ____________________ of me to not show up at faculty meetings and to not grade papers.
7. Having to walk three days through the savanna with little food or water was a(n) ____________________ experience.
8. Ingrid was ____________________ that finishing her education in classical Greek literature was necessary for her career.
9. Matteo felt ____________________ after spending fourteen hours moving the family into their new home.
10. Often tyrants see themselves as a(n) ____________________ leader with much more clout than anyone else.

Lesson 63

LIFE GOES ON

Festivities in the village were about to **commence**. The village square was packed with half-drunken peasants who were shouting loudly and creating a scene of total **bedlam**. The mayor had organized a carnival night in order to **divert** the villagers' attention from the recent tragedy in which a forest fire destroyed a part of the crop, for he knew that some jollity would **motivate** the peasants to overcome their grief and find solutions to the issue. Certainly a night of thoughtless enjoyment was most **welcome** for the anxious peasants.

NEW WORDS

bedlam
ˈbedləm

divert
diˈvərt, dī-

commence
kəˈmens

motivate
ˈmōtəˌvāt

welcome
ˈwelkəm

Definitions: Try matching the words in the list with the appropriate definitions. If you are stuck, check the glossary in the back of the book or the passage at the top of the page.

1.	bedlam	__________	a.	a scene of uproar and confusion
2.	divert	__________	b.	1. to cause someone or something to change course or turn from one direction to another; 2. to distract someone or his or her attention from something
3.	commence	__________	c.	1. to provide someone with an objective for doing something; 2. to stimulate one's interest in doing something
4.	motivate	__________	d.	(adj.) (of a guest or new arrival) gladly received; (n.) an instance or manner of greeting someone; (v.) 1. to greet someone arriving in a glad or friendly way; 2. to react with pleasure or approval to an event or development
5.	welcome	__________	e.	to begin, start

Sentences: Try to use the words above in a sentence below. Remember that a word ending may be changed or its figure of speech slightly altered.

6. It is difficult to ____________________ someone who has no interest in doing a task.
7. The fall semester will ____________________ in the second week of September.
8. When the lighting crew and actors started quarreling with each other, ____________________ broke out on stage.
9. Alexis tried to ____________________ her parents' attention away from discussing the family vacation by demanding that she be fed immediately.
10. Guests at the new hotel feel ____________________ as soon as the friendly staff get their bags, give them complimentary cookies, and show them a lovely, clean room.

Lesson 64

NEW WORDS

audacious
ô'dāSHəs

residual
ri'zijo͞oəl

magnetic
mag'netik

acclaim
ə'klām

aloof
ə'lo͞of

A LIFE-CHANGING ACCIDENT

Jack used to possess a **magnetic** personality and was thus able to engage anyone he met in banter and jokes. However, after he made the **audacious** move to shield a child from a horse-drawn carriage breaking loose, Jack was badly wounded. The great **acclaim** he received from the police department for his bravery was not enough to compensate for his physical injuries. Having to travel around in wheelchairs and to tolerate the **residual** pain after his knee surgery, Jack turned into a cranky and **aloof** person. He even severed ties with his old friends, as they became a painful reminder of his prime youth.

Definitions: Try matching the words in the list with the appropriate definitions. If you are stuck, check the glossary in the back of the book or the passage at the top of the page.

1.	audacious	__________	a.	(adj.) remaining after the greater part is gone; (n.) the remaining amount after other things have been subtracted or allowed for
2.	residual	__________	b.	(n.) enthusiastic public praise; (v.) to praise enthusiastically and publicly
3.	magnetic	__________	c.	not friendly or forthcoming; cold; distant
4.	acclaim	__________	d.	1. showing a willingness to take bold risks; 2. showing an impudent lack of respect
5.	aloof	__________	e.	(adj.) 1. capable of being attracted by or acquiring the properties of a magnet; 2. very attractive or alluring

Sentences: Try to use the words above in a sentence below. Remember that a word ending may be changed or its figure of speech slightly altered.

6. The new musical has received much ____________________ in recent weeks from the press, who are hailing it as one of the most impressive pieces of this generation.
7. Benjamin was ____________________ at the party: he stood in the corner and kept to himself instead of socializing with the guests.
8. Everyone loved Talya's ____________________ personality: they were drawn to her charismatic charm, her wonderful caring nature, and her exciting stories.
9. Sales from my books furnish me a(n) ____________________ income on top of my hourly salary.
10. The ____________________ employee called out his boss' ethical mishaps and resigned on the spot.

Lesson 65

THE AMBITIOUS NEWCOMER

The **novice** at the design studio was extremely diligent and full of **vim** and inner strength. A desire to learn and succeed would **infuse** every task he performed. Even when his supervisor gave him a project of **colossal** proportions, the beginner worked hard to finish it before the deadline. It seemed that nothing could **thwart** his efforts to progress in the workplace as fast as possible.

NEW WORDS

colossal
kəˈläsəl

thwart
THwôrt

novice
ˈnävəs

infuse
inˈfyo͞oz

vim
vim

Definitions: Try matching the words in the list with the appropriate definitions. If you are stuck, check the glossary in the back of the book or the passage at the top of the page.

1.	colossal	__________	a.	extremely large
2.	thwart	__________	b.	to fill or pervade; to instill a quality in someone or something
3.	novice	__________	c.	energy; enthusiasm
4.	infuse	__________	d.	to prevent someone from accomplishing something; to stymie
5.	vim	__________	e.	a person who is new or inexperienced in a field or situation

Sentences: Try to use the words above in a sentence below. Remember that a word ending may be changed or its figure of speech slightly altered.

6. Lena is so full of ____________________ that she has done a week's work in eleven hours!
7. The evil villain tried to ____________________ the hero from rescuing his princess but failed in every attempt.
8. Sid is a(n) ____________________ at sailing; he lacks deep experience in how to navigate a boat at sea.
9. The ricotta cheese in that cannoli is ____________________ with orange rinds and citrus flavor.
10. That pumpkin is ____________________: it is at least five times larger than any I've seen before and it must weigh a ton!

NEW WORDS

versatile
ˈvərsətl

quaint
kwānt

instigate
ˈinstiˌgāt

rue
ro͞o

rectify
ˈrektəˌfī

Lesson 66

THE ENTREPRENEURIAL MAN

A man of **versatile** talents, John decided to leave his career in writing to start a woodworking business. He had always been interested in redecorating **quaint** old furniture that was sold in antique shops. He was not good at bargaining, however, and ultimately lost all of his money. That caused him to **rue** his decision to get into the new business. He wanted to **rectify** the situation but he did not know how to pay off all his debts. His financial troubles were enough to **instigate** him to try something brand new – to get into the cooking industry – which ultimately brought him much financial success and personal satisfaction.

Definitions: Try matching the words in the list with the appropriate definitions. If you are stuck, check the glossary in the back of the book or the passage at the top of the page.

1. versatile ________ a. to bring about or initiate an action or event; to provoke
2. quaint ________ b. (n.) repentance, regret, compassion, or pity; (v.) to bitterly regret
3. instigate ________ c. able to adapt to many different functions or activities
4. rue ________ d. attractively unusual or old-fashioned, often resembling small town or rustic life
5. rectify ________ e. to set something right; to correct

Sentences: Try to use the words above in a sentence below. Remember that a word ending may be changed or its figure of speech slightly altered.

6. Nothing could be done to ________________ Giao's deplorable behavior in school.
7. Heath will ________________ the day that he tells his wife he wants a divorce.
8. Someone who is ________________ can adapt to many different situations because he or she has a broad skill set.
9. Compared to city life in Los Angeles, life in in the rural Ohio town of Sandusky seemed pretty ________________.
10. Joanna ________________ school reform when she complained that she was discriminated against based on the clothing she was wearing.

Lesson 67

HITCH YOUR WAGON TO A STAR

Stewie and Steven had been friends since childhood, and remained so even after Steven became an accomplished fencer and moved out of town. Their friendship lasted in part because Stewie found that there is a positive **correlation** between one's success as a professional athlete and that person's ability to **inspire** and motivate others to achieve their personal goals. Thankfully, Steven's success did not estrange him from Stewie. Just the other day, Steven picked up the phone to offer Stewie advice on how to **differentiate** between a correctly executed **lunge** and a bad one. Stewie found his friend's initiative **laudable**.

NEW WORDS

differentiate
ˌdifəˈrenSHēˌāt

lunge
lənj

inspire
inˈspīr

laudable
ˈlôdəbəl

correlation
ˌkôrəˈlāSHən

Definitions: Try matching the words in the list with the appropriate definitions. If you are stuck, check the glossary in the back of the book or the passage at the top of the page.

1.	differentiate ________	a.	a mutual relationship or connection between two or more things
2.	lunge ________	b.	to recognize or figure out what makes something different
3.	inspire ________	c.	(n.) a sudden forward thrust of the body typically to attack someone or to seize something; (v.) to make a sudden forward thrust with a part of the body or a weapon
4.	laudable ________	d.	to fill someone with the urge or ability to feel or do something
5.	correlation ________	e.	praiseworthy; commendable

Sentences: Try to use the words above in a sentence below. Remember that a word ending may be changed or its figure of speech slightly altered.

6. A good teacher not only educates students, but also ____________________ them to be better people.
7. The fencer ____________________ at his opponent and scored a point.
8. There is little or no ____________________ between a person's height and his or her intelligence.
9. It is hard to ____________________ between the two sample shades of blue in which my room will be painted.
10. Tony's performance was ____________________, and he received due praise from the audience for acting so well.

NEW WORDS

rancid
ˈransid

wealth
welTH

surly
ˈsərlē

revel
ˈrevəl

apparent
əˈparənt, əˈpe(ə)r-

Lesson 68

RICH AND UNHAPPY

James was a handsome and well-educated young man who had no **apparent** reason to be unhappy with his life. What is more, he had inherited great **wealth** from his parents and was able to **revel** in luxury. However, after his girlfriend ran away with his butler, James became unbearably **surly**. One morning he fired a servant only because the latter supposedly served him **rancid** bacon for breakfast. After that incident, everyone in the house became scared of him.

Definitions: Try matching the words in the list with the appropriate definitions. If you are stuck, check the glossary in the back of the book or the passage at the top of the page.

1.	rancid	________	a.	an abundance of valuable possessions or money; plentiful supplies of a particular resource
2.	wealth	________	b.	bad-tempered and unfriendly
3.	surly	________	c.	clearly visible or true, obvious; seemingly true
4.	revel	________	d.	(of foods) smelling or tasting unpleasant as a result of being old or stale
5.	apparent	________	e.	to enjoy oneself in a noisy and lively way; to delight in

Sentences: Try to use the words above in a sentence below. Remember that a word ending may be changed or its figure of speech slightly altered.

6. It is ____________________ that Blake does not want to be at the meeting because he keeps staring around the room paying attention to nothing.
7. You should discuss your research project with Lester, for he has a(n) ____________________ of knowledge on the topics you are studying.
8. The milk in the refrigerator tasted ____________________ and needed to be thrown out.
9. Gianna ____________________ in the excitement of the annual risotto festival.
10. A child who is ____________________ throws tantrums and often cries uncontrollably.

Lesson 69

THE AFFABLE HOST

Watching a culinary show every Saturday morning did much to **kindle** Matthew's interest in cooking. He knew that he would **thrive** in a job that allowed him to experiment and to make people happy. After he became a chef, he started a successful cooking show of his own. He was an **affable** host and was well liked by the public because if his pleasing personality. For instance, once he cut himself with a knife and did not even **wince**; he just continued smiling. Another time he was late for a live broadcast of his show and decided to **atone** for being late by handing everyone in the audience invitations for a free dinner at his restaurant.

NEW WORDS

kindle
ˈkindl

thrive
THrīv

atone
əˈtōn

affable
ˈafəbəl

wince
wins

Definitions: Try matching the words in the list with the appropriate definitions. If you are stuck, check the glossary in the back of the book or the passage at the top of the page.

1.	kindle	________	a.	(n.) a slight grimace or recoiling caused by pain or distress; (v.) to grimace, shake, or recoil as the result of pain or distress
2.	thrive	________	b.	friendly, easy to talk to, good-natured
3.	atone	________	c.	to flourish; to grow vigorously
4.	affable	________	d.	to make amends or reparation
5.	wince	________	e.	to light or set on fire; to arouse or inspire

Sentences: Try to use the words above in a sentence below. Remember that a word ending may be changed or its figure of speech slightly altered.

6. Fido is a(n) ____________________ dog and thus loves greeting and playing with visitors.
7. Irene went to the temple to ____________________ for her sins and to seek spiritual support in overcoming her troubles.
8. Dominique's interest in French literature was ____________________ after she saw *Les Miserables* performed at the theater when she was twelve.
9. Dolores ____________________ when she received the injection because she hates the sight and pain of receiving shots.
10. Generally, molds ____________________ in damp places that are sufficiently warm and moist.

NEW WORDS

abbreviate
ə'brēvē͵āt

gullible
'gələbəl

coach
kōCH

wayward
'wāwərd

obligate
'äbli͵gāt

Lesson 70

THE DIFFICULT CHILD

Lord Conley's youngest son, Andrew, caused him much trouble. The **wayward** child would obey neither his father's commands nor the rules of the house. The child's tennis **coach**, for example, complained that Andrew skipped most of his practices. His poetry teacher claimed that Andrew had such a short attention span that the former needed to **abbreviate** his lectures because the boy would not listen. By creating more strict rules for Andrew, Lord Conley tried to **obligate** him to behave better. Andrew was not **gullible**, however. He knew that Lord Conley was not really a disciplinarian and that he could get away with anything – despite having new strict rules imposed on him.

Definitions: Try matching the words in the list with the appropriate definitions. If you are stuck, check the glossary in the back of the book or the passage at the top of the page.

1.	abbreviate	________	a.	credulous; easily persuaded to believe something
2.	gullible	________	b.	(1.) a horse-drawn or motor carriage; 2. a railway car; 3. an athletic instructor or trainer; (v.) to instruct or train athletes
3.	coach	________	c.	difficult to predict or control because of unusual or perverse behavior
4.	wayward	________	d.	to shorten a word, phrase, or text
5.	obligate	________	e.	to require, especially legally or morally

Sentences: Try to use the words above in a sentence below. Remember that a word ending may be changed or its figure of speech slightly altered.

6. These guidelines do not ____________________ you to work a minimum of forty hours per week, but we strongly recommend that you do so.
7. One may ____________________ the word "California" merely by writing "CA" on a document.
8. The ____________________ unified the rugby team and helped them win nine games in a row, thus taking them to the championship.
9. The ____________________ priest took the Church charity contributions and spent them on a luxury Caribbean vacation.
10. Often children are so ____________________ that they will believe anything you tell them, so it is best to use strong words to force them to do their work.

Crossword Puzzle

Lessons 61-70

ACROSS

4 (adj.) remaining after the greater part is gone; (n.) the remaining amount after other things have been subtracted or allowed for
5 (adj.) (of foods) smelling or tasting unpleasant as a result of being old or stale
8 (v.) 1. to cause someone or something to change course or turn from one direction to another; 2. to distract someone or his or her attention from something
10 (v.) to shorten a word, phrase, or text
12 (adj.) lacking care or attention to duty; negligent
15 (v.) to recognize or figure out what makes something different
18 (n.) a person who is new or inexperienced in a field or situation
19 (v.) to make amends or reparation
20 (adj.) 1. showing a willingness to take bold risks; 2. showing an impudent lack of respect

DOWN

1 (v.) to light or set on fire; to arouse or inspire
2 (v.) 1. to provide someone with an objective for doing something; 2. to stimulate one's interest in doing something
3 (adj.) credulous; easily persuaded to believe something
6 (n.) a mutual relationship or connection between two or more things
7 (n.) an abundance of valuable possessions or money; plentiful supplies of a particular resource
9 (v.) to bring about or initiate an action or event; to provoke
11 (n.) superior to all others; strongest, most important, or most powerful; very great or intense
13 (n.) repentance, regret, compassion, or pity; (v.) to bitterly regret
14 (adj.) accompanying but not a major part of something
16 (adj.) forming, existing on, or related to the outside of something; (n.) the outer surface or structure of something
17 (v.) to fill or pervade; to instill a quality in someone or something

Vocabulary Review
Lessons 61-70

Directions: Match each word with its best approximate definition. Note that definitions are not necessarily repeated verbatim from the lesson exercises.

1.	stalemate	________	a.	obvious; clearly visible or understood
2.	dynamic	________	b.	to prevent someone from accomplishing something; to oppose a plan, attempt, or ambition successfully
3.	adamant	________	c.	extremely distressing
4.	harrowing	________	d.	to fill someone with the urge or drive to do something
5.	bedlam	________	e.	alluring; attractive; capable of attracting things
6.	commence	________	f.	refusing to be persuaded to change one's mind
7.	magnetic	________	g.	a scene of great confusion or uproar
8.	aloof	________	h.	characterized by constant change, activity, or progress
9.	colossal	________	i.	extremely large
10.	thwart	________	j.	to begin
11.	versatile	________	k.	to grow or develop well or vigorously
12.	rectify	________	l.	an involuntary grimace or movement in response to anticipating pain
13.	inspire	________	m.	a draw; a position where neither opponent can make progress successfully
14.	laudable	________	n.	able to adapt to many circumstances
15.	surly	________	o.	unfriendly or ill-tempered
16.	apparent	________	p.	difficult to control or predict because of perverse behavior
17.	thrive	________	q.	to correct or put something right
18.	wince	________	r.	praiseworthy
19.	wayward	________	s.	to compel someone legally or morally
20.	obligate	________	t.	not friendly or forthcoming; cool and distant

Word Roots: Unit 7

ROOTS AND THEIR MEANINGS

retro:	**backward, behind**	**simil/simul:**	**likeness, imitation**
cis:	**to cut**	**am:**	**to love**
urb:	**city**	**co/com/con:**	**with, together**

Here are a few examples of some words that use the above roots:

retrograde:	movement that is directed backward
scissors:	implement or instrument used to cut materials
urban:	concerning or relating to a city or a town
simultaneous:	occurring, happening, or operating at the same time
amorous:	showing, feeling, or relating to sexual desire
connect:	to join together so that a link (either literally or figuratively) is established

Now try to fill in the table below by finding the appropriate root(s) and interpreting the meaning of each word:

Word	Root(s)	Guessed Meaning	Actual Meaning
simulate			
combine			
retroactive			
cooperate			
retrospect			
amicable			
suburbia			
incision			

Lesson 71

NEW WORDS

ostracize
ˈästrəˌsīz

rankle
ˈraNGkəl

pragmatic
pragˈmatik

indict
inˈdīt

hovel
ˈhəvəl, ˈhävəl

ANNOYING ERIN

After trying to **rankle** her high school classmates on many occasions, Erin found that not many people wanted to be her friend. Classmates would **ostracize** her at school events and make her feel unwelcome at parties and concerts. Because of this, she often sat in her **hovel** crying for hours on end. In an attempt to be **pragmatic**, Erin attempted to apologize for her irritating behavior. But that was to no avail. Her classmates said that although there was no broken law, they wished that someone could **indict** her on account of being rude. Unfortunately, the rift between Erin and her school friends persisted and Erin could not form new friendships until she went to college.

Definitions: Try matching the words in the list with the appropriate definitions. If you are stuck, check the glossary in the back of the book or the passage at the top of the page.

1.	ostracize	__________	a.	to exclude someone from a group or society
2.	rankle	__________	b.	to cause persistent irritation, annoyance, or resentment
3.	pragmatic	__________	c.	a small and squalid dwelling
4.	indict	__________	d.	practical; sensible; realistic
5.	hovel	__________	e.	to formally accuse or charge with a serious crime

Sentences: Try to use the words above in a sentence below. Remember that a word ending may be changed or its figure of speech slightly altered.

6. Members of the department chose to ____________________ the student because he did not fit in with the rest of the team.
7. After a long investigative process, the criminal finally was ____________________ for grand theft auto.
8. Jenny was ____________________ by the new policies that the company had enacted; she no longer had freedom to do the things that she used to enjoy.
9. Julius was sick of living in a(n) ____________________ and so spent his life savings on a brand new luxury condominium.
10. It is ____________________ to study subjects that will help you obtain a good job in the future.

Lesson 72

OPENING UP

Catherine was known as a harsh and irritable woman. It was easy to **deplete** her patience when working with children. Her usual icy glare, however, began to **thaw** when she first met her niece, Elly. Catherine's affection became more evident as time went on. Although she was often exasperated if anyone interrupted her in the middle of work, Catherine would spend time helping Elly **polish** her essays or play with her dolls even when she was drowning in work. Catherine simply could not refuse any **favor** Elly asked, no matter how **absurd**.

NEW WORDS

absurd
əbˈsərd, -ˈzərd

favor
ˈfāvər

polish
ˈpäliSH

deplete
diˈplēt

thaw
THô

Definitions: Try matching the words in the list with the appropriate definitions. If you are stuck, check the glossary in the back of the book or the passage at the top of the page.

1.	absurd	________	a.	to use up the supply or resources of
2.	favor	________	b.	(n.) an attitude of approval or liking; 2. an act of kindness beyond what is due or necessary; (v.) to show approval or preference for
3.	polish	________	c.	(n.) a substance that gives an object a smooth and shiny surface when the latter is rubbed; (v.) to make the surface of something smooth and shiny by rubbing it
4.	deplete	________	d.	(usually of ice or snow) to become liquid or soft as a result of warming
5.	thaw	________	e.	wildly ridiculous, insensible, or foolish

Sentences: Try to use the words above in a sentence below. Remember that a word ending may be changed or its figure of speech slightly altered.

6. If an army ____________________ its resources during war, it likely will suffer defeat.
7. It is important to let a frozen piece of meat ____________________ before cooking it.
8. To think that you can jump out of a window and fly through the air is ____________________: humans have no wings and were not meant to fly.
9. Each week the maid would come and ____________________ the silver tea set in our kitchen.
10. My brother did me a(n) ____________________ and bought me dinner because he knew I was broke.

Lesson 73

NEW WORDS

swagger
ˈswagər

retribution
ˌretrəˈbyo͞oSHən

annihilate
əˈnī-əˌlāt

bloated
ˈblōtid

discretion
disˈkreSHən

THE VICIOUS GANGSTER

Everything about the new gang leader demanded respect. He walked with a **swagger** and spoke with an authoritative voice. He threatened to **annihilate** all competition from other local gangs. His leadership style was marked by violence and brutal **retribution** for any act of betrayal. The new leader also desired constant admiration from his gang members in order to satisfy his **bloated** ego. He never used **discretion** when dealing with guilty gang members; in fact, it seemed to give him much pleasure to publicly humiliate others.

Definitions: Try matching the words in the list with the appropriate definitions. If you are stuck, check the glossary in the back of the book or the passage at the top of the page.

1.	swagger	________	a.	to destroy completely; to obliterate
2.	retribution	________	b.	1. (of the body) swollen with fluid or gas; 2. excessive in size or amount
3.	annihilate	________	c.	the quality of behaving in such a way that offence is not caused or private information is not revealed
4.	bloated	________	d.	(n.) a confident, arrogant, or aggressive walk; (v.) to walk in a confident, arrogant, or aggressive way
5.	discretion	________	e.	punishment inflicted on someone as vengeance for a wrong or criminal act

Sentences: Try to use the words above in a sentence below. Remember that a word ending may be changed or its figure of speech slightly altered.

6. When the United States dropped an atomic bomb on Hiroshima in 1945, much of the city was immediately ____________________.
7. Regina felt ____________________ after having eaten a pot of chicken soup, a plate of spaghetti, and two pieces of chocolate cake.
8. It is important to use ____________________ when speaking to people of authority, because they may hold sway over your future.
9. Astrid walked with a(n) ____________________ of authority, and the people in her office respected her for having so much command over her work.
10. The mafia boss killed his cousin's wife as ____________________ for the latter squealing on his illicit business.

Lesson 74

QUEST FOR TREASURE

Guided by a **personable** local, Josh and Emily finally arrived at the **grotto** that was rumored to be where a 13th-century pirate buried his treasure. Emily always showed **unconditional** support for her husband's decisions, but she was uncertain this time. The grotto looked beautiful yet ominous, reminding her of the rumors about the deathly curses on anyone who coveted the treasure. Emily was sure she saw something floating in the dark, but Josh dismissed her assertion as an **illusion**. No matter how much she tried to **implore** him to leave, Josh was determined to enter.

NEW WORDS

implore
imˈplôr

personable
ˈpərsənəbəl

grotto
ˈgrätō

illusion
iˈlo͞oZHən

unconditional
ˌənkənˈdiSHənl, -ˈdiSHnəl

Definitions: Try matching the words in the list with the appropriate definitions. If you are stuck, check the glossary in the back of the book or the passage at the top of the page.

1. implore __________ a. to beg someone earnestly to do something
2. personable __________ b. a small picturesque cave, especially a fake one in a garden or park
3. grotto __________ c. (of a person) having a pleasant manner or appearance
4. illusion __________ d. not subject to any stipulations or limitations
5. unconditional ________ e. a thing that is likely to be wrongly perceived by the senses; a deception; a false idea or belief

Sentences: Try to use the words above in a sentence below. Remember that a word ending may be changed or its figure of speech slightly altered.

6. My father ____________________ me not to marry the girl I had been dating for two years; he said she was almost certainly a bad match for me.
7. A parent's love for his or her child should be ____________________.
8. I appreciate working with others who are ____________________, for they make the banalities of a job seem bearable.
9. Please tell me how that magician created the ____________________ of being able to fly!
10. The lovers nestled in the ____________________ and discussed their future together.

Lesson 75

NEW WORDS

inevitable
in'evitəbəl

astute
ə'st(y)o͞ot

concise
kən'sīs

desolate
'desəlit

abrogate
'abrə,gāt

FOREIGN WORKERS

As the economy got worse and business shrank, it was **inevitable** that the company would lay people off. The firm decided to **abrogate** its contracts with its international workers. This was an **astute** fiscal move since the company had to pay much smaller severance packages to these workers than to domestic working citizens. The company gave the international workers a **concise** explanation of why they were being laid off and demanded that the workers leave the premises immediately. Most of the workers depended fully on their job and felt completely **desolate**. They did not know how they would survive in a foreign country without a job.

Definitions: Try matching the words in the list with the appropriate definitions. If you are stuck, check the glossary in the back of the book or the passage at the top of the page.

1.	inevitable	__________	a.	deserted of people and in a state of bleak and dismal emptiness
2.	astute	__________	b.	certain to occur; unavoidable
3.	concise	__________	c.	giving much information in few words
4.	desolate	__________	d.	having the ability to accurately assess situations or people and turn them to one's advantage
5.	abrogate	__________	e.	to repeal or do away with a law, right, or formal agreement

Sentences: Try to use the words above in a sentence below. Remember that a word ending may be changed or its figure of speech slightly altered.

6. Death is one part of existence that is ____________________: in the end all people will eventually pass away.
7. Berna was very ____________________ and realized from the business figures that her partners were secretly pocketing company profit for themselves.
8. It is better to write a speech that is ____________________ than to write one that rambles and is longwinded.
9. To me, Antarctica seems like a(n) ____________________ place; there are few other humans there and nothing but penguins and a barren ice-covered landscape to see.
10. It is important not to ____________________ your responsibilities as a parent.

Lesson 76

LIFE ON THE STREETS

The homeless children would **forage** the streets for food during the night. Now that their father was in prison, they needed to have much **fortitude** in order to survive alone. During the day, shopkeepers yelled at them and other children on the streets would **imitate** the grown ups and scream and make faces at them. This filled the homeless children with **indignation.** The world seemed to be an unjust place full of rejection and violence softened only by **accidental** acts of kindness that happened very rarely.

NEW WORDS

forage
ˈfôrij, ˈfär-

fortitude
ˈfôrtəˌto͞od

accidental
ˌaksiˈdentl

indignation
ˌindigˈnāSHən

imitate
ˈimiˌtāt

Definitions: Try matching the words in the list with the appropriate definitions. If you are stuck, check the glossary in the back of the book or the passage at the top of the page.

1.	forage	__________	a.	courage in pain or adversity
2.	fortitude	__________	b.	happening by chance, unintentionally, or unexpectedly
3.	accidental	__________	c.	to take or follow as a model; to copy someone else's mannerisms; to copy or simulate
4.	indignation	__________	d.	anger or annoyance caused by what is perceived as unfair treatment
5.	imitate	__________	e.	to search widely for food or provisions

Sentences: Try to use the words above in a sentence below. Remember that a word ending may be changed or its figure of speech slightly altered.

6. We watched the deer ____________________ for food in the woods behind our home.
7. It takes great emotional ____________________ to flourish in the wake of a parent's passing.
8. It was purely ____________________ that Tony found himself in Manhattan on Valentine's Day: he flew to New York for a business meeting only after his boss suddenly had fallen ill.
9. When students learn a foreign language, they often ____________________ their instructor's sounds and gestures.
10. Lee experienced an outburst of ____________________ from her employer after she failed to complete her job responsibilities in a timely and professional manner.

NEW WORDS

devout
di'vout

frequent
'frēkwənt

strategy
'stratəjē

prologue
'prō,lôg, -,läg

sanction
'saNG(k)SHən

Lesson 77

THE LOCAL PREACHER

Mr. White's introductory speech was the **prologue** to a long evening of lectures. As a **devout** churchgoer, Mr. White believed that it was his duty to spread the word of the gospel to everyone. He organized **frequent** dinners at his restaurant for the local community. Offering free meals was his **strategy** for accomplishing his goal. The people who attended such dinners were usually the poorest in the neighborhood. They knew that Mr. White would only **sanction** discussions on religious matters and they accepted that as long as there was free food.

Definitions: Try matching the words in the list with the appropriate definitions. If you are stuck, check the glossary in the back of the book or the passage at the top of the page.

1.	devout	________	a.	having or showing deep religious feeling or commitment
2.	frequent	________	b.	(n.) 1. a threatened penalty for disobeying a law or rule; 2. official approval or permission for an action; (v.) 1. to give official approval or permission for an action; 2. to impose a penalty on
3.	strategy	________	c.	a plan of action or policy designed with a specific aim
4.	prologue	________	d.	(adj.) 1. occurring on many occasions, often, or habitual; 2. occurring in short distances apart; (v.) to visit a place often or habitually
5.	sanction	________	e.	an introductory section of a literary work or musical piece

Sentences: Try to use the words above in a sentence below. Remember that a word ending may be changed or its figure of speech slightly altered.

6. One cannot win a battle easily if one lacks a(n) ________________ to defeat one's opponent.
7. As a(n) ________________ Catholic, I go to church every Sunday.
8. The author explained his intellectual motivations and thanked his colleagues for their support in the book's ________________.
9. I ________________ the restaurant, as it serves an excellent turkey dinner with stuffing and mashed potatoes.
10. The airline company does not ________________ employees taking photographs of themselves or others in uniform.

Lesson 78

DISENCHANTED ATTORNEY

Robert was known for throwing **ostentatious** parties at his villa. And while luxury cars, designer outfits, and exquisite hors d'oeuvres were **plentiful** at such events, Robert hardly felt excited or even **neutral** about such gatherings. He loathed them and felt constrained. Robert hoped to one day **liberate** himself from the social elites with whom he needed to associate in his career as a prominent lawyer. How he wished to live in a society where social climbing was **defunct**, where people would judge others based on their character and not on their salary or pedigree! One day, he thought, it would happen.

NEW WORDS

plentiful
ˈplentəfəl

liberate
ˈlibəˌrāt

defunct
diˈfəNGkt

ostentatious
ˌästənˈtāSHəs

neutral
ˈn(y)o͞otrəl

Definitions: Try matching the words in the list with the appropriate definitions. If you are stuck, check the glossary in the back of the book or the passage at the top of the page.

1. plentiful ________ a. no longer existing or functioning
2. liberate ________ b. existing in great quantity; abundant
3. defunct ________ c. 1. not helping or supporting either side in a conflict; 2. having no strongly marked positive or biased characteristics; 3. (physics) neither positively nor negatively charged; 4. (chemistry) neither acid nor alkaline
4. ostentatious ________ d. characterized by pretentious display meant to attract attention
5. neutral ________ e. to set someone free from a situation (esp. slavery or imprisonment); to free one from a situation that limits free thought or expression or has rigid social conventions; to free from enemy occupation

Sentences: Try to use the words above in a sentence below. Remember that a word ending may be changed or its figure of speech slightly altered.

6. Unfortunately the beautiful train station is now ________________: tourists can take pictures of it from afar, but they cannot access it or catch a train there.
7. The singer showed up, as usual, with a(n) ________________ entry: four individuals dressed as sentries carried her in on a pallet.
8. Rather than taking sides in an argument, I prefer to remain ________________.
9. The prisoner obtained keys to all of the jail cells and unlocked them in an effort to ________________ all of the inmates.
10. There is always ________________ food at the Thanksgiving buffet; you should go check it out!

Lesson 79

NEW WORDS

exorbitant
ig'zôrbitənt

perceptive
pər'septiv

elderly
'eldərlē

acquire
ə'kwī(ə)r

squalid
'skwälid

THE NEW LEADER

After capturing the Commanding General, the enemy locked him up in a **squalid** prison, and intended to acquire an **exorbitant** ransom. Given these circumstances, a new leader needed to be elected to launch a counter-attack and to rescue the Commanding General. Lieutenant General Foster was the most viable selection. Although he was **elderly**, Foster was far more **perceptive** and courageous than his younger comrades. Over the years that he had served in the army, Foster also managed to **acquire** a reputation for never losing in battle, no matter how perilous the situation was.

Definitions: Try matching the words in the list with the appropriate definitions. If you are stuck, check the glossary in the back of the book or the passage at the top of the page.

1.	exorbitant	________	a.	a price or amount charged that is unreasonably high
2.	perceptive	________	b.	1. a place that is filthy and unpleasant, usually because of neglect or poverty; 2. exhibiting a lack of moral standards
3.	elderly	________	c.	1. to buy or obtain an object; 2. to learn or develop a specific skill or skill set; 3. to achieve a reputation as a result of one's behavior or activity
4.	acquire	________	d.	exhibiting sensitive insight
5.	squalid	________	e.	a person who is old or showing signs of aging

Sentences: Try to use the words above in a sentence below. Remember that a word ending may be changed or its figure of speech slightly altered.

6. The price of a hamburger at this restaurant is ________________: is costs more than six times what it would cost at any other eatery.
7. A(n) ________________ person would have been able to sense that his boss was seeking to start a new life and career elsewhere.
8. Only through hard and sustained work can one ________________ enough money to take an early retirement.
9. If your parents knew you were living in such ________________ conditions, they would demand that you move to a new home.
10. Every week, Stacey volunteers her time to help ________________ people cook and go shopping.

Lesson 80

FAMILIAL TRANSFORMATION

The parents were worried about their son, who had become very **belligerent** and verbally aggressive after the bullying incident at school. Every loud noise would **render** the boy very nervous and angry. The family got together to **ponder** how to help him become more relaxed. They decided to **accentuate** the boy's feeling of security by giving him daily hugs and telling him that he was safe. As a result of the boy's trauma, the communication in the family increased, which seemed to have a good effect on the father as well. A long-time alcoholic, the father began to show **temperance** in his alcohol consumption and started to spend more evenings with his son.

NEW WORDS

ponder
ˈpändər

accentuate
akˈsenCHo͞oˌāt

render
ˈrendər

belligerent
bəˈlijərənt

temperance
ˈtemp(ə)rəns

Definitions: Try matching the words in the list with the appropriate definitions. If you are stuck, check the glossary in the back of the book or the passage at the top of the page.

1.	ponder	__________	a.	hostile and aggressive
2.	accentuate	__________	b.	to make more prominent or noticeable
3.	render	__________	c.	1. to provide or give a service or help; 2. to cause to become or make; 3. to represent or depict artistically
4.	belligerent	__________	d.	moderation or self-restraint, especially from drinking
5.	temperance	__________	e.	to think carefully about something before making a decision

Sentences: Try to use the words above in a sentence below. Remember that a word ending may be changed or its figure of speech slightly altered.

6. The artist was unskilled and thus unable to ____________________ my image very well, painting a terrible portrait of me.
7. That striped shirt can ____________________ your stomach and make you look chubby.
8. The ____________________ athlete threatened to beat up the coach after the team lost the basketball match.
9. Often in philosophy class, I would ____________________ the meaning of justice.
10. Alma exhibited ____________________ in ending her relationship: she politely told her boyfriend that she wanted to stop dating without becoming overemotional about matters.

Word Search

Lessons 71-80

O S T E N T A T I O U S Q Q R W T

E T Q U Q N L W R M M B M M P L G

X N B G M T K L Z E M E I Z K M E

O E M O B I K M T T R N T L Y L Y

R U O L M M N A L O E W J J K Y Y

B Q S O Y B U D L V J L N N L B D

I E T R E T D P I K M O A R Y J Y

T R R P N T M T B G I R F N D R G

A F A E L I A L M T N O R J G R T

N M C D J B O G U D R A E V O J W

T C I W L A M B O T L R T T D Q Z

A R Z E T Q I R I R I A T I G Y D

T P E E B R N T K U B O B T O J Y

X V D D T M U J Q M E A D S H N J

Y J J E N D D C B K R M V Q U A B

R X R Q E O A T D T A D M Y D R W

K K M R Y R P X W T T D N J G R D

B M Q D W J M B M J E W M R G Y B

1 (v.) to exclude someone from a group or society
2 (v.) to cause persistent irritation, annoyance, or resentment
3 (adj.) wildly ridiculous, insensible, or foolish
4 (v.) (usually of ice or snow) to become liquid or soft as a result of warming
5 (n.) punishment inflicted on someone as vengeance for a wrong or criminal act
6 (adj.) 1. (of the body) swollen with fluid or gas; 2. excessive in size or amount
7 (v.) to beg someone earnestly to do something
8 (n.) a small picturesque cave, especially a fake one in a garden or park
9 (adj.) certain to occur; unavoidable
10 (v.) to repeal or do away with a law, right, or formal agreement
11 (n.) courage in pain or adversity
12 (n.) anger or annoyance caused by what is perceived as unfair treatment
13 (adj.) 1. occurring on many occasions, often, or habitual; 2. occurring in short distances apart; (v.) to visit a place often or habitually
14 (n.) an introductory section of a literary work or musical piece
15 (v.) to set someone free from a situation (esp. slavery or imprisonment); to free one from a situation that limits free thought or expression or has rigid social conventions; to free from enemy occupation
16 (adj.) characterized by pretentious display meant to attract attention
17 (adj.) a price or amount charged that is unreasonably high
18 (v.) 1. to buy or obtain an object; 2. to learn or develop a specific skill or skill set; 3. to achieve a reputation as a result of one's behavior or activity
19 (v.) to think carefully about something before making a decision
20 (v.) to make more prominent or noticeable

Vocabulary Review
Lessons 71-80

Directions: Match each word with its best approximate definition. Note that definitions are not necessarily repeated verbatim from the lesson exercises.

1.	indict	________	a.	a plan of action designed to achieve an overall aim
2.	hovel	________	b.	abundant
3.	favor	________	c.	brief but comprehensive
4.	deplete	________	d.	hostile and aggressive; combative
5.	swagger	________	e.	an act of kindness beyond what is necessary; to show preference for
6.	annihilate	________	f.	a thing that is likely to be wrongly interpreted by the senses
7.	personable	________	g.	to destroy completely; to obliterate
8.	illusion	________	h.	having sensitive insight
9.	astute	________	i.	no longer existing or functioning
10.	concise	________	j.	concerning a person with a pleasant appearance and manner
11.	forage	________	k.	(of a person); concerning being old or aging
12.	accidental	________	l.	a small, squalid dwelling
13.	devout	________	m.	to walk or behave in a confident or arrogant way
14.	strategy	________	n.	for a person or animal to search widely for food or provisions
15.	plentiful	________	o.	to use up the supply or resources of something
16.	defunct	________	p.	having a keen ability to assess people or situations and to turn this to one's advantage
17.	perceptive	________	q.	to formally accuse or charge with a serious crime
18.	elderly	________	r.	moderation and self restraint (usually concerning food and drink)
19.	belligerent	________	s.	not deliberate; happening by chance
20.	temperance	________	t.	having or showing deep commitment (often religiously)

Literary and Drama Terms

Whether you have a passion for literature or you feel forced to learn it for exams, there are terms that you should know. Below is a list of major literary terms that will help you better understand how literature operates.

alliteration:	**the use of the same letter or sound at the beginning of adjacent or nearly connected words**
analogy:	**a comparison between two things, usually for the purpose of instruction or clarification**
anecdote:	**a short, catchy story about an intriguing incident or person**
eulogy:	**a speech or writing that praises someone excessively, often after that person's death**
foreshadow:	**something that serves as a warning or indication of a future event**
hyperbole:	**claims or statements that are so exaggerated as to not be able to be taken literally in a serious manner**
irony:	**a set of affairs or circumstances that seems to be the exact opposite of what one would expect, thus resulting in amusement or empathy**
foil (n.):	**a character or object used for contrast in order to emphasize and enhance the qualities of another**

metaphor: a figure of speech where a word or phrase is applied to an action to which it cannot in reality or literally be applied; a thing that is regarded as symbolic or representative of something else

onomatopoeia: the use of a word that sounds exactly like its name (e.g. ding dong, boom, cuckoo)

personification: the attribution of human characteristics to something that is nonhuman; giving some abstract entity humanlike attributes

plot: the main events of a novel, play, or other work presented in some form of sequence

pseudonym: a fictitious name used by an author of a work, almost always because the author does not want to reveal his or her identity

setting: the place and time in which a novel, short story, play, or other event takes place

simile: a figure of speech comparing one thing with another using "like" or "as" in the comparison

soliloquy: often used in a play, the act of speaking or reading one's feelings aloud – regardless of whether other people are present

synopsis: a brief summary of a piece of writing, drama, film, or other piece of art

NEW WORDS

panorama
ˌpanəˈramə, -ˈrämə

monarch
ˈmänərk, ˈmänˌärk

desecrate
ˈdesiˌkrāt

heterogeneous
ˌhetərəˈjēnēəs

tortuous
ˈtôrCHo͞oəs

Lesson 81

REGRETTING THE PAST

Looking out at the majestic **panorama** of his empire, the **monarch** lamented on his past. After years of battles, he finally united and ruled over many culturally **heterogeneous** lands. However, during this **tortuous** process, he also lost many of his friends, subordinates, and even family members. He made countless enemies as well, for during his conquest, the monarch employed cruel tactics, such as attempting to **desecrate** churches and temples, and to massacre people ruthlessly. Now, at the peak of his power, he somehow felt lost.

Definitions: Try matching the words in the list with the appropriate definitions. If you are stuck, check the glossary in the back of the book or the passage at the top of the page.

1.	panorama __________	a.	twisting or winding
2.	monarch __________	b.	to treat something sacred with disrespect
3.	desecrate __________	c.	a sovereign head of state such as a king, queen, or emperor
4.	heterogeneous ______	d.	1. an unbroken view of a whole region surrounding an observer; 2. a complete survey or presentation of a sequence of events or a subject
5.	tortuous __________	e.	diverse in content or in character

Sentences: Try to use the words above in a sentence below. Remember that a word ending may be changed or its figure of speech slightly altered.

6. The compassionate ______________________ ruled over his subjects with concern and care.
7. Gangs attempted to ______________________ the monument by painting all over it with graffiti.
8. One can view a(n) ______________________ of the city from the top of the mountain.
9. As Josh hurriedly drove up the ______________________ mountain road, I became nauseous from all the twists and turns.
10. Next year's graduating class will be the most ______________________ ever: it will contain students from over fifty countries, and have people of various creeds and races.

Lesson 82

THE INJURED SPORTSMAN

After the tennis player suffered a **contusion** on the arm, he had to withdraw from the competition. The injury came at a very inconvenient moment since the player had just received a **barrage** of requests to attend different tournaments. His physiotherapists did their best to **amend** the situation; however, there was not much to do except wait for the wound to heal. Nevertheless, the player exhibited good **etiquette** and formally apologized to the tournament director and the public, vowing to make his **comeback** as soon as possible.

NEW WORDS

amend
əˈmend

barrage
bəˈräZH

etiquette
ˈetikit, -ˌket

comeback
ˈkəmˌbak

contusion
kənˈto͞oZHən

Definitions: Try matching the words in the list with the appropriate definitions. If you are stuck, check the glossary in the back of the book or the passage at the top of the page.

1.	amend	________	a.	(n.) a concentrated outpouring or firing of something; (v.) to bombard someone with something
2.	barrage	________	b.	the customary code of appropriate behavior in society; manners
3.	etiquette	________	c.	to modify or make better, more accurate, or up-to-date by implementing small changes in something
4.	comeback	________	d.	a bruise
5.	contusion	________	e.	1. a return by a well-known person to the field in which they were originally successful; 2. a quick reply to a critical remark

Sentences: Try to use the words above in a sentence below. Remember that a word ending may be changed or its figure of speech slightly altered.

6. The doctor asked the patient about the ____________________ on her arm.
7. After decades of being unpopular, it seems that disco and swing dancing are making a(n) ____________________.
8. It is difficult to ____________________ the business articles without a vote of approval from the board of directors.
9. The politician was confronted with a(n) ____________________ of questions from journalists after news broke that he had been instrumental in a giant property scandal.
10. It is important to display proper ____________________ at the ceremony so that you can show how well mannered you are.

NEW WORDS

indicate
'indi͵kāt

nebula
'nebyələ

enhance
en'hans

surrogate
'sərəgit, -͵gāt

callous
'kaləs

Lesson 83

A WONDERFUL TEACHER

After parents found out that Mr. Freinster forced his students to slap each other as punishment for not doing homework, this **callous** teacher was quickly fired. Mr. Nelson, a new science teacher, became his **surrogate**, and the students instantly loved him. The broad and genuine smile on his face appeared to **indicate** how much he enjoyed teaching, which was a stark contrast to Mr. Freinster's ever-present grumpy expression. Mr. Nelson also prepared engaging materials, organized fun games and activities, and even took the class on a field trip to the planetarium to **enhance** his lectures on galaxies and how a **nebula** forms.

Definitions: Try matching the words in the list with the appropriate definitions. If you are stuck, check the glossary in the back of the book or the passage at the top of the page.

1. indicate __________ a. a substitute, especially another person deputizing for another in a specific role or office
2. nebula __________ b. exhibiting an insensitive and cruel disregard for others
3. enhance __________ c. to intensify, increase, or improve the quality of
4. surrogate __________ d. 1. a cloud of gas in outer space; 2. any bright spot in the night sky
5. callous __________ e. 1. to point out or show; to briefly state something; to gesture; to show or register a reading (of a meter or gauge); 2. to suggest or show signs of a necessary course of action

Sentences: Try to use the words above in a sentence below. Remember that a word ending may be changed or its figure of speech slightly altered.

6. Is would be ____________________ to tell someone on crutches that he or she needs to take the stairs in lieu of the elevator to get to work.
7. That hazy blob you see through the telescope is a(n) ____________________.
8. Helping the poor children at the pagoda will not only ____________________ your résumé but also make you feel better about yourself.
9. A guardian often serves as a(n) ____________________ parent for a child.
10. Trong's grades seem to ____________________ that he is not studying very well in school.

Lesson 84

THE ANNOYING LANDLADY

The old widow Spencer made her living from renting rooms to young university students. She had many rules and made **repetitive** visits to each **boarder** to check on each room. She was also **dogmatic** and loved to regularly instruct the young people about how they should live their lives, which the boarders found annoying and **redundant**. After all, she was only a landlady and their housing agreements did not **specify** that they needed to meet with her on a daily basis and listen to her lectures. It seemed that both parties had different ideas about the nature of their relationship.

NEW WORDS

specify
ˈspesəˌfī

repetitive
riˈpetətiv

boarder
ˈbôrdər

dogmatic
dôgˈmatik

redundant
riˈdəndənt

Definitions: Try matching the words in the list with the appropriate definitions. If you are stuck, check the glossary in the back of the book or the passage at the top of the page.

1.	specify	__________	a.	inclined to lay down principles as absolute truth
2.	repetitive	__________	b.	1. superfluous; no longer needed to be useful or functioning; 2. words or data that can be omitted without loss of meaning
3.	boarder	__________	c.	characterized by doing something over and over again or something happening over and over again often in a tiresome way
4.	dogmatic	__________	d.	a person (often a student residing at school) who receives regular meals when staying somewhere
5.	redundant	__________	e.	to identify or state a fact clearly and definitely

Sentences: Try to use the words above in a sentence below. Remember that a word ending may be changed or its figure of speech slightly altered.

6. Miss Smith has a rather ____________________ approach to English pedagogy: she asserts that the only way to learn to write is by composing five paragraph essays every week for a year.
7. Without further information on the guest list, I am unable to ____________________ whether I want to serve chicken or pasta at the rehearsal dinner.
8. The worker found that drilling holes in wooden planks all day was a(n) ____________________ task, so he quit his job and looked for new employment.
9. When writing a concise and proper sentence it is necessary to omit ____________________ information.
10. The preparatory school down the road has over two hundred ____________________ who study there.

Lesson 85

NEW WORDS

inauspicious
ˈinôˈspiSHəs

mitigate
ˈmitəˌgāt

inhabit
inˈhabit

founder
ˈfoundər

effect
iˈfekt

RAGS TO RICHES

Olivia had quite an **inauspicious** childhood. As a penniless orphan, she grew up in a slum that rats and insects would also **inhabit**, and often got bullied by the neighborhood kids. However, these negative experiences had no **effect** on her dreams of becoming a fashion designer – Olivia still persistently worked towards her goals. With her creativity and talent, Olivia has now become the **founder** and owner of a successful fashion shop. She even donates part of her shop's profits to local charity programs, hoping to **mitigate** the poverty and crime in her old neighborhood.

Definitions: Try matching the words in the list with the appropriate definitions. If you are stuck, check the glossary in the back of the book or the passage at the top of the page.

1. inauspicious ________
2. mitigate ________
3. inhabit ________
4. founder ________
5. effect ________

a. (of a person or animal) to live in a particular place or geographic region
b. to make less painful, serious, or severe
c. (n.) a person who establishes a business, organization, club, or institution; (v.) (usually of a ship) to fill with water and sink
d. unfavorable; unpromising
e. (n.) 1. a change that is the result of another action or cause; 2. the extent to which something succeeds or is operative; 3. an impression produced in the mind of a person; (v.) to cause something to happen or bring about

Sentences: Try to use the words above in a sentence below. Remember that a word ending may be changed or its figure of speech slightly altered.

6. Little could ____________________ the pain Gloria felt after losing her husband in a boating accident.
7. Many elephants ____________________ the lush, flat land of Sri Lanka.
8. I am unsure what ____________________ the new medicine will have on Rehana; hopefully it will make her a happier person!
9. After a few ____________________ months, Ratan closed up his Bengali restaurant.
10. After three canons hit the sloop, the boat began to ____________________ and its crew departed in lifeboats.

Lesson 86

THE MAN WHO FELT NO PAIN

The old man, who had been injured in a fire, had a big **lesion** on his thigh. He seemed to be in much pain but dismissed it in a **debonair** manner. Instead of complaining, he would recite to himself a **stanza** or two from his favorite poems while waiting for the doctors to apply some medicine on the wound. While the other victims of the fire would beg and **plead** for more painkillers, the old man seemed to be in a state of complete **tranquility**, as if he did not notice the pain.

NEW WORDS

debonair
ˌdebəˈne(ə)r

lesion
ˈlēZHən

stanza
ˈstanzə

plead
plēd

tranquility
ˌtraNGˈkwilitē

Definitions: Try matching the words in the list with the appropriate definitions. If you are stuck, check the glossary in the back of the book or the passage at the top of the page.

1.	debonair	__________	a.	1. to present an emotional appeal or to beg; 2. to present and argue for a particular position in a public context, especially a court
2.	lesion	__________	b.	(of a man) stylish, charming, and confident
3.	stanza	__________	c.	part of tissue or an organ that has suffered a cut, wound, ulcer, or abscess
4.	plead	__________	d.	a group of lines forming the basic metrical unit of a poem
5.	tranquility	__________	e.	calmness; serenity; peacefulness

Sentences: Try to use the words above in a sentence below. Remember that a word ending may be changed or its figure of speech slightly altered.

6. Gary took early retirement because work was unsettling and he felt that he needed more ____________________ in his life.
7. Floyd looked ____________________ at last night's dinner: the tuxedo together with his charisma made him a real charmer!
8. Though the first four were easy to write, I am having trouble writing the final ____________________ of this poem.
9. A child should not have to ____________________ with his or her parents to receive love and attention.
10. While in triage, the nurse asked Stevie about the nature of the ____________________ on her waist.

NEW WORDS

prolific
prə'lifik

submerge
səb'mərj

dissemble
di'sembəl

innate
i'nāt

fallow
'falō

Lesson 87

THE TWISTS AND TURNS OF LIFE

James prided himself on being a **prolific** writer who produced at least two books a year. He would **submerge** himself totally in the creative process and write for days on end. However, his mother's death had a profound effect on him. James tried to **dissemble** his grief but it was obvious that he was no longer the same person. He seemed to have lost his **innate** ability to write continuously. His talent and his creative abilities would lie **fallow** for a very long period after his personal tragedy.

Definitions: Try matching the words in the list with the appropriate definitions. If you are stuck, check the glossary in the back of the book or the passage at the top of the page.

1.	prolific	__________	a.	inborn or natural
2.	submerge	__________	b.	1. a plant animal or person producing much fruit, foliage, or offspring; 2. an author, artist, or composer who produces a great deal; 3. present in large numbers or quantities
3.	dissemble	__________	c.	1. to place under water or some other liquid; 2. to completely cover or obscure
4.	innate	__________	d.	farmland that is ploughed and harrowed but left uncultivated to restore its fertility for crop production
5.	fallow	__________	e.	to conceal one's true intentions, beliefs, or feelings

Sentences: Try to use the words above in a sentence below. Remember that a word ending may be changed or its figure of speech slightly altered.

6. Rather than being honest with his family, the child chose to ____________________ his responses to their questions.
7. Ahmad is a(n) ____________________ writer; he has written over a dozen papers and books on Islamic culture in the past decade.
8. Many people argue that mathematical ability is ____________________: one either is born with it or lacks it.
9. The goal of a submarine is to ____________________ itself in the ocean so that others cannot easily find it.
10. The farmer left a quarter of his field ____________________ in order to let it rejuvenate with fresh minerals for next year's planting.

Lesson 88

REACHING SUCCESS

Edmond was regarded as an excellent juggler and an agile, **kinetic** performer. He also had an **amiable** personality, which appealed to the public. However, he went unnoticed by big entertainment companies for years. Finally, he was invited to take part in the national dance academy's **jubilee**, the most important event of the year for the dance community. Edmond was honored by the invitation; for him it marked an **epoch** of social success in his life. With unparalleled **valor** he attempted some very difficult acts, which involved juggling objects that were set on fire. He was determined to make a great impression.

NEW WORDS

amiable
ˈāmēəbəl

epoch
ˈepək

jubilee
ˈjo͞obəˌlē, ˌjo͞obəˈlē

kinetic
kəˈnetik

valor
ˈvalər

Definitions: Try matching the words in the list with the appropriate definitions. If you are stuck, check the glossary in the back of the book or the passage at the top of the page.

1.	amiable	__________	a.	of, concerning, or relating to motion
2.	epoch	__________	b.	a period of time in one's life or in a historical period marked by notable events; (geology) a long time period that is divided into ages
3.	jubilee	__________	c.	courage in the face of danger
4.	kinetic	__________	d.	a special anniversary of an event (especially 25 years, 50 years, etc.)
5.	valor	__________	e.	friendly and pleasant

Sentences: Try to use the words above in a sentence below. Remember that a word ending may be changed or its figure of speech slightly altered.

6. Scholars have often referred to the ____________________ between Nicolaus Copernicus (1473-1543) and Isaac Newton (1643-1727) as the "Scientific Revolution," a time when rapid and unprecedented developments in mathematics, physics, and the natural sciences were made.
7. Proponents of a(n) ____________________ theory of learning believe that students achieve the best results when they are active.
8. There is a(n) ____________________ celebrating the fiftieth anniversary of the pharmacy.
9. The knight was praised for his ____________________ in protecting the kingdom from being attacked by trolls and ogres.
10. Humphrey is a(n) ____________________ person who enjoys talking to others and learning about their lives.

Lesson 89

NEW WORDS

vanquish
ˈvaNGkwiSH

declamation
ˌdekləˈmāSHən

ample
ˈampəl

conciliate
kənˈsilēˌāt

schism
ˈs(k)izəm

JOINING EFFORTS

After the Civil War started, the country fell into a state of tumult, with economic inflation, political riots, and constant battles between the two main warring parties. A right-wing politician, Vasili, knew that this **schism** would only give neighboring countries **ample** opportunity to start attacking. With the current vulnerable state of the country, it would be easy for its enemies to **vanquish** the army and get control of the government. Vasili thus delivered a passionate **declamation** to **conciliate** the left wing and warn it of the impending danger.

Definitions: Try matching the words in the list with the appropriate definitions. If you are stuck, check the glossary in the back of the book or the passage at the top of the page.

1.	vanquish	__________	a.	a split or division between strongly opposed parties or groups within a party caused by differences of opinion or belief
2.	declamation	__________	b.	to defeat thoroughly
3.	ample	__________	c.	a speech delivered in a rhetorical or passionate way
4.	conciliate	__________	d.	enough or more than enough; large and plentiful; large and accommodating
5.	schism	__________	e.	to stop someone from being angry; to placate; to pacify

Sentences: Try to use the words above in a sentence below. Remember that a word ending may be changed or its figure of speech slightly altered.

6. A(n) ____________________ within the corporation resulted in the company breaking into two different divisions with different visions and leadership.
7. Ronald gave a bitter ____________________ on the folly of using torture on one's enemies.
8. Harlow could do little to ____________________ his friends after their mother grounded them for a month.
9. There are ____________________ cookies in the pantry so nobody will be left hungry or wanting.
10. The baseball team ____________________ its opponent in the playoffs and then proceeded to the finals.

Lesson 90

THE ESCAPE

Poetry created for Jonas an **ethereal** world of beautiful images where he could escape from his daily life. This is because Jonas found the dramatic poetic realm to be strikingly different from his routine job, in which he would often sit behind his desk in a **torpid** state. Reading poetry kept his mind engaged and prevented him from becoming **obtuse.** Poetry was his escape from the **pathology** of his office life, which consisted of long working hours combined with monotonous tasks. Often Jonas would become **ecstatic** upon discovering the work of a new poet.

NEW WORDS

ethereal
iˈTHi(ə)rēəl

ecstatic
ekˈstatik

torpid
ˈtôrpid

pathology
pəˈTHäləjē

obtuse
əbˈt(y)o͞os, äb-

Definitions: Try matching the words in the list with the appropriate definitions. If you are stuck, check the glossary in the back of the book or the passage at the top of the page.

1.	ethereal	__________	a.	1. annoyingly insensitive or slow to understand; 2. an angle whose measure is greater than 90 degrees and less than 180 degrees
2.	ecstatic	__________	b.	the science of the causes and effects of disease
3.	torpid	__________	c.	feeling overwhelming joy or excitement
4.	pathology	__________	d.	1. feeling too light or delicate for the world; 2. heavenly or spiritual
5.	obtuse	__________	e.	mentally or physically exhaustive; lethargic

Sentences: Try to use the words above in a sentence below. Remember that a word ending may be changed or its figure of speech slightly altered.

6. One who is ____________________ typically lacks the energy to run for office.
7. Uma was ____________________ when she heard that she was admitted to her first-choice college.
8. Having spent years engrossed in ____________________, the physician believed he could find a cure for cancer.
9. Keith, a practical man, could not relate to the ____________________ discussion that the professors were having at the dinner table.
10. Only a(n) ____________________ student would not understand how basic multiplication works.

Crossword Puzzle

Lessons 81-90

ACROSS

3 (n.) 1. a cloud of gas in outer space; 2. any bright spot in the night sky
5 (adj.) of, concerning, or relating to motion
7 (v.) to modify or make better, more accurate, or up-to-date by implementing small changes in something
11 (v.) 1. to place under water or some other liquid; 2. to completely cover or obscure
12 (n.) the science of the causes and effects of disease
13 (v.) to stop someone from being angry; to placate; to pacify
15 (n.) a sovereign head of state such as a king, queen, or emperor
16 (adj.) twisting or winding
19 (adj.) 1. feeling too light or delicate for the world; 2. heavenly or spiritual
20 (n.) a person who establishes a business, organization, club, or institution; (v.) (usually of a ship) to fill with water and sink

DOWN

1 (n.) a concentrated outpouring or firing of something; (v.) to bombard someone with something
2 (v.) to make less painful, serious, or severe
4 (adj.) 1. a plant animal or person producing much fruit, foliage, or offspring; 2. an author, artist, or composer who produces a great deal; 3. present in large numbers or quantities
6 (adj.) exhibiting an insensitive disregard for others
8 (adj.) characterized by doing something over and over again or something happening over and over again in a tiresome way
9 (adj.) (of a man) stylish, charming, and confident
10 (adj.) enough or more than enough; large and plentiful; large and accommodating
14 (n.) a person (often a student residing at school) who receives regular meals when staying somewhere
17 (n.) courage in the face of danger
18 (n.) a group of lines forming the basic metrical unit of a poem

Vocabulary Review
Lessons 81-90

Directions: Match each word with its best approximate definition. Note that definitions are not necessarily repeated verbatim from the lesson exercises.

1.	desecrate	________	a.	to intensify, increase, or further improve the value of
2.	heterogeneous	________	b.	peacefulness, calmness
3.	etiquette	________	c.	to defeat thoroughly
4.	contusion	________	d.	a bruise
5.	indicate	________	e.	inborn, natural
6.	enhance	________	f.	the customary code of behavior in society; manners
7.	specify	________	g.	diverse in character or content
8.	dogmatic	________	h.	given to setting down principles as incontrovertibly true
9.	inauspicious	________	i.	feeling overwhelming happiness or joy and excitement
10.	inhabit	________	j.	a special anniversary of an event
11.	lesion	________	k.	concerning farmland left unused or uncultivated in order to restore its fertility for crop production
12.	tranquility	________	l.	a speech given in a rhetorical or impassioned manner
13.	innate	________	m.	to identify definitely and clearly
14.	fallow	________	n.	a region in an organ or tissue that has suffered damage through disease
15.	amiable	________	o.	unpromising; not conducive to success
16.	jubilee	________	p.	to treat a sacred ting with violent disrespect
17.	vanquish	________	q.	physically or mentally inactive; lethargic
18.	declamation	________	r.	to live in or occupy a place or environment
19.	ecstatic	________	s.	having or showing a friendly disposition
20.	torpid	________	t.	to point out, to show; to suggest a necessary course of action

Specific Vocabularies 2
Government and Legal Words

Government Terms:

- A **president** leads the United States of America
- **Congress** refers to the legislative body of the United States government; it is composed of both the **Senate** and the **House of Representatives**
- A **senator** is an individual representing his or her state in the Senate
- A **representative** is an individual representing his or her district in the **House of Representatives**
- A **governor** is in charge of running a state
- A **mayor** is in charge of running a city
- An **alderman** is an elected member of a municipal council
- The term **gubernatorial** refers to things related to a governor or the office of a governor
- The term **municipal** refers to things related to city government

Courtroom and Legal Terms:

- A **judge** is a person who presides over a courtroom
- A **magistrate** is a civil office or lay judge who administers the law in minor cases
- A **felony** is a serious crime, usually involving violence and punishable by over a year in prison or death
- A **misdemeanor** is a minor offense or wrongdoing
- A **plaintiff** is a person who brings a case against another in a court of law
- A **defendant** is an individual, company, or institution that is accused in a court of law
- A **bailiff** is a person in a court of law who keeps order and who looks after prisoners

ANSWER KEY

Lesson 1

1. d
2. b
3. c
4. a
5. e
6. intellectual
7. fickle
8. embrace
9. generalize
10. diligent

Lesson 2

1. d
2. e
3. b
4. c
5. a
6. optimal
7. waxed
8. noisome
9. beneficial
10. encumber

Lesson 3

1. e
2. b
3. c
4. d
5. a
6. accrue
7. enthralled
8. ruddy
9. disposition
10. celestial

Lesson 4

1. e
2. a
3. d
4. b
5. c
6. hasten
7. manipulate
8. linchpin
9. enlighten
10. erroneous

Lesson 5

1. d
2. e
3. c
4. b
5. a
6. glossed
7. weather
8. lithe
9. scarce
10. praise

Lesson 6

1. e
2. c
3. d
4. b
5. a
6. mendicant
7. resuscitate
8. ferocious
9. warp
10. endeavoring

Lesson 7

1. a
2. d
3. c
4. e
5. b
6. blend
7. harsh
8. theoretical
9. articulate
10. convene

Lesson 8

1. d
2. e
3. b
4. c
5. a
6. caliber
7. raze
8. incurred
9. antisocial
10. relish

Lesson 9

1. c
2. b
3. d
4. e
5. a
6. egress
7. graphic
8. deliberating
9. ignoble
10. imminent

Lesson 10

1. c
2. e
3. a
4. b
5. d
6. candid
7. summit
8. extravagant
9. alternate
10. mar

Crossword Puzzle: Lessons 1-10

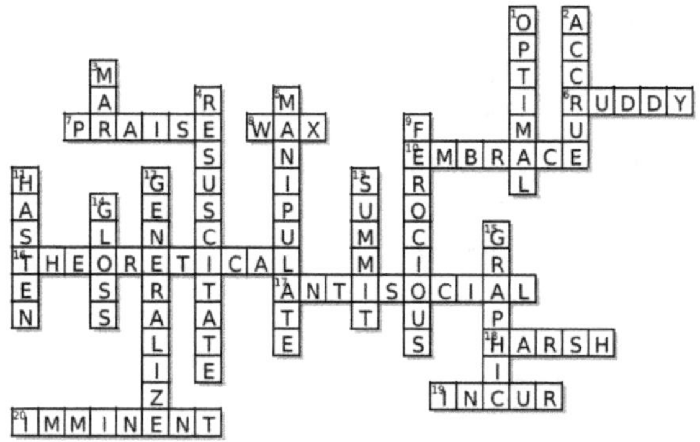

Review: Lessons 1-10

1. t
2. k
3. i
4. p
5. g
6. f
7. c
8. a
9. n
10. h
11. o
12. e
13. b
14. l
15. j
16. r
17. s
18. q
19. d
20. m

Lesson 11

1. b
2. a
3. e
4. d
5. c
6. variance
7. vague
8. reception
9. deficiency
10. kiln

Lesson 12

1. d
2. c
3. a
4. b
5. e
6. noxious
7. ambulatory
8. notice
9. bland
10. predicament

Lesson 13

1. d
2. b
3. a
4. c
5. e
6. heirloom
7. instantaneously
8. pathetic
9. pose
10. forlorn

Lesson 14

1. c
2. e
3. d
4. a
5. b
6. akin
7. suffice
8. predecessor
9. juncture
10. tacit

Lesson 15

1. d
2. b
3. a
4. c
5. e
6. yield
7. cloned
8. conspicuous
9. bard
10. repress

Lesson 16

1. d
2. b
3. a
4. c
5. e
6. vouch
7. erratic
8. innumerable
9. galactic
10. aghast

Lesson 17

1. c
2. d
3. a
4. b
5. e
6. tumult
7. lore
8. adroit
9. arbitrator
10. retract

Lesson 18

1. d
2. a
3. e
4. b
5. c
6. herculean
7. merger
8. abashed
9. antidote
10. inclination

Lesson 19

1. a
2. b
3. d
4. e
5. c
6. iniquity
7. pigment
8. conduit
9. brevity
10. shirk

Lesson 20

1. c
2. b
3. d
4. a
5. e
6. grant
7. drone
8. convey
9. priceless
10. prevaricate

Word Search: Lessons 11-20

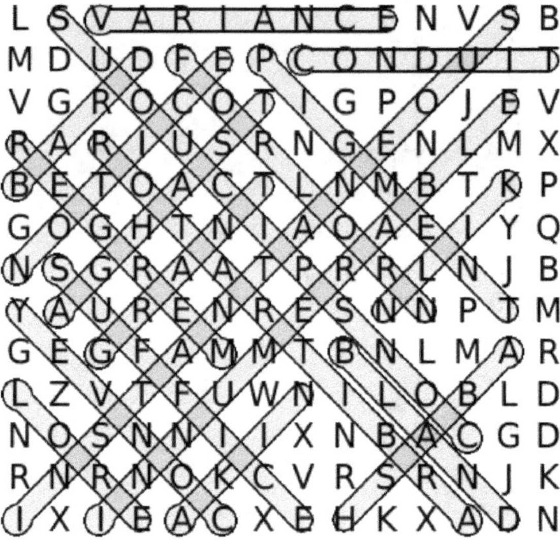

Review: Lessons 11-20

1. t
2. s
3. m
4. f
5. k
6. n
7. r
8. a
9. h
10. j
11. g
12. o
13. b
14. q
15. l
16. p
17. d
18. c
19. i
20. e

Lesson 21

1. a
2. d
3. e

4. b
5. c
6. oration
7. illustrate
8. additional
9. detrimental
10. impudent

Lesson 22

1. b
2. a
3. c
4. e
5. d
6. incoherent
7. brusque
8. recognize
9. lexicon
10. paltry

Lesson 23

1. c
2. a
3. d
4. b
5. e
6. margin
7. patron
8. mores
9. joyous
10. opinion

Lesson 24

1. a
2. d
3. e
4. b
5. c
6. gainsay
7. goodwill
8. buffet
9. facile
10. scalpel

Lesson 25

1. d
2. e
3. a
4. c
5. b
6. newfangled
7. discreet
8. frivolous
9. operate
10. collaborate

Lesson 26

1. b
2. e
3. c
4. d
5. a
6. evacuate
7. ascertain
8. solid
9. objectionable
10. extol

Lesson 27

1. e
2. d
3. c
4. b
5. a
6. oasis
7. splendid
8. repudiated
9. unilateral
10. buffer

Lesson 28

1. e
2. d
3. a
4. b
5. c
6. copious

7. traumatic
8. fanatic
9. negative
10. effectual

Lesson 29

1. d
2. b
3. c
4. e
5. a
6. scourge
7. entity
8. convenient
9. fiasco
10. dose

Lesson 30

1. a
2. e
3. d
4. b
5. c
6. warrant
7. strive
8. ruptured
9. vogue
10. wan

Crossword Puzzle: Lessons 21-30

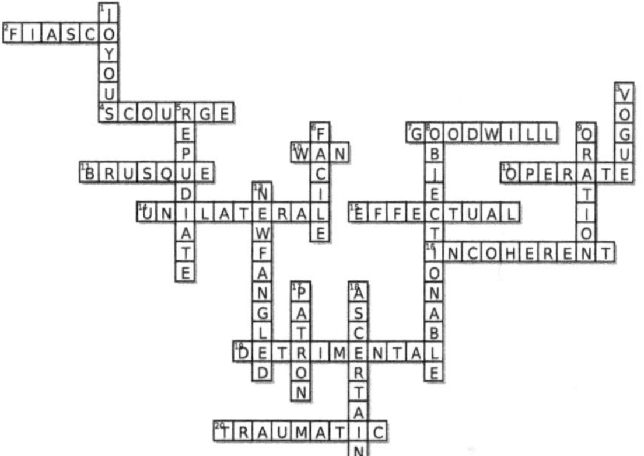

Review: Lessons 21-30

1. m
2. n
3. j
4. t
5. q
6. g
7. i
8. f
9. h
10. b
11. k
12. c
13. r
14. p
15. d
16. a
17. l
18. o
19. e
20. s

Lesson 31

1. c
2. a
3. b
4. e
5. d
6. incision
7. pompous
8. scoured
9. ingenious
10. shrewd

Lesson 32

1. d
2. c
3. b
4. a
5. e
6. menial
7. pursuit
8. fidelity
9. usurp
10. gourmand

Lesson 33

1. c
2. b
3. e
4. a
5. d
6. acquiesced
7. choreography
8. incorrigible
9. laceration
10. grovel

Lesson 34

1. a
2. c
3. b
4. d
5. e
6. appliance
7. atrocity
8. euphoria
9. frock
10. nomad

Lesson 35

1. a
2. c
3. e
4. b
5. d
6. detour
7. memento
8. illegible
9. migrated
10. rendezvous

Lesson 36

1. c
2. b
3. e
4. d
5. a
6. blasphemy
7. malevolent
8. rebuffed
9. subsidy
10. levity

Lesson 37

1. a
2. e
3. c
4. d
5. b
6. flabbergasted
7. idiom
8. fling
9. famine
10. clash

Lesson 38

1. a
2. d
3. c
4. e
5. b
6. amass
7. cavity
8. ruffled
9. constant
10. cling

Lesson 39

1. c
2. b
3. d
4. e
5. a
6. despondent
7. prior
8. policy
9. amorphous
10. protrudes

Lesson 40

1. c
2. e
3. a
4. b
5. d
6. ominous
7. prevalent
8. portly
9. fretful
10. approval

Word Search: Lessons 31-40

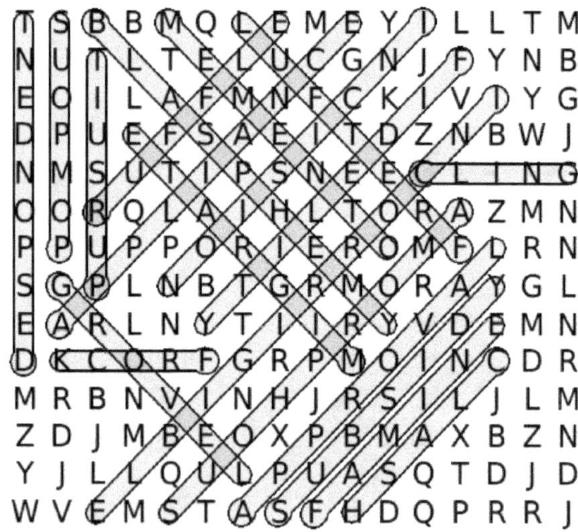

Review: Lessons 31-40

1. d
2. i
3. o
4. a
5. q
6. h
7. f
8. g
9. r
10. n
11. m
12. l
13. j
14. s
15. e
16. p
17. t
18. b
19. k
20. c

Lesson 41

1. c
2. a
3. b
4. d
5. e
6. trade
7. simulate
8. distress
9. aggrandize
10. culpable

Lesson 42

1. a
2. c
3. b
4. d
5. e
6. restitution
7. succumbed
8. intercepted
9. craft
10. annulled

Lesson 43

1. c
2. e
3. b
4. d
5. a
6. domicile
7. arid
8. culture
9. retorted
10. arrogant

Lesson 44

1. c
2. b
3. d
4. a
5. e
6. encountered
7. wary
8. benevolent
9. demonstrate
10. berated

Lesson 45

1. d
2. c
3. a
4. b
5. e
6. undermines
7. ardor
8. dutiful
9. credulous
10. trekked

Lesson 46

1. e
2. b
3. a
4. c
5. d
6. nucleus
7. crisis
8. sate
9. prosperous
10. congenial

Lesson 47

1. c
2. a
3. b
4. d
5. e
6. strenuous
7. flux
8. pungent
9. dogged
10. obliged

Lesson 48

1. a
2. d
3. e
4. c
5. b
6. blueprint
7. fluctuate
8. prolong
9. inspect
10. basis

Lesson 49

1. e
2. c
3. d
4. a
5. b
6. pacifist
7. severe
8. prey
9. authentic
10. deplore

Lesson 50

1. e
2. d
3. b
4. c
5. a
6. acquaintance
7. initiate
8. muster
9. voluminous
10. covert

Crossword Puzzle: Lessons 41-50

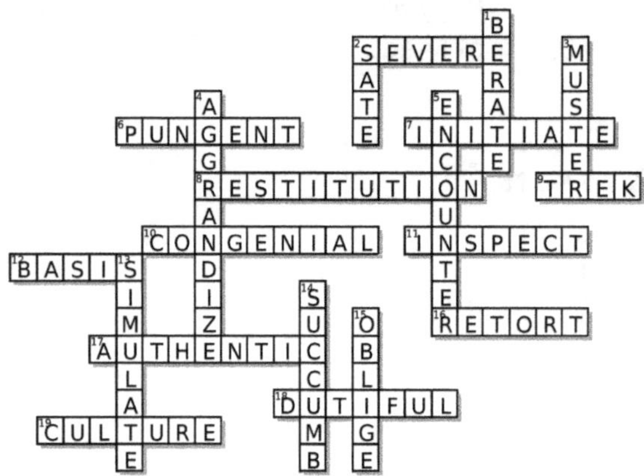

Review: Lessons 41-50

1. l
2. n
3. q
4. h
5. f
6. i
7. c
8. t
9. p
10. a
11. g
12. m
13. d
14. j
15. b
16. k
17. e
18. s
19. o
20. r

Lesson 51

1. a
2. e
3. c
4. d
5. b
6. mute
7. universally
8. adversity
9. adorn
10. marvel

Lesson 52

1. a
2. d
3. c
4. b
5. e
6. irrational
7. eccentric
8. beverage
9. sabbatical
10. unruly

Lesson 53

1. a
2. d
3. c
4. e
5. b
6. amalgamation
7. feat
8. vulnerable
9. alleviate
10. gesture

Lesson 54

1. d
2. e
3. b
4. c
5. a
6. fissure
7. jubilant
8. election
9. miscellaneous
10. synopsis

Lesson 55

1. b
2. e
3. d
4. c
5. a
6. authoritarian
7. mandatory
8. ailment
9. deluged
10. underlying

Lesson 56

1. e
2. a
3. d
4. c
5. b
6. spontaneous
7. rejuvenate
8. transact
9. gregarious
10. humble

Lesson 57

1. c
2. e
3. a
4. d
5. b
6. triumph
7. timorous
8. transparent
9. cavort
10. incited

Lesson 58

1. b
2. c
3. d
4. e
5. a
6. vex
7. custom
8. timid
9. rife
10. quench

Lesson 59

1. d
2. e
3. b
4. c
5. a
6. verify
7. mundane
8. exquisite
9. suspend
10. magnitude

Lesson 60

1. a
2. c
3. e
4. d
5. b
6. amity
7. physiognomy
8. focal
9. sequential
10. accumulate

Word Search: Lessons 51-60

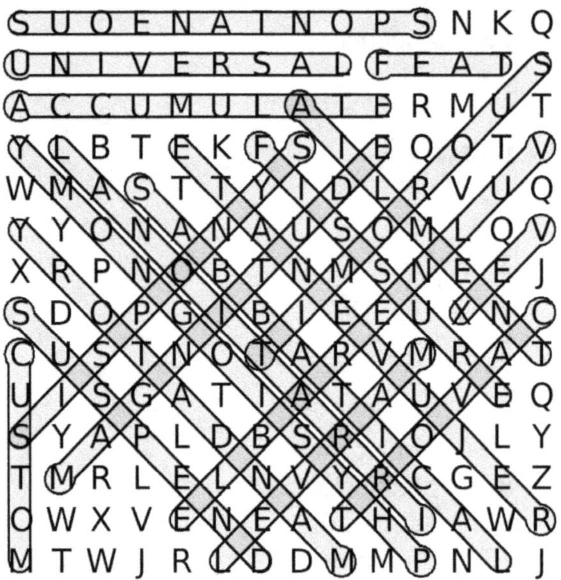

Review: Lessons 51-60

1. q
2. t
3. d
4. k
5. l
6. e
7. f
8. o
9. s
10. i
11. h
12. m
13. j
14. c
15. a
16. p
17. r
18. g
19. b
20. n

Lesson 61

1. e
2. d
3. a
4. c
5. b
6. exterior
7. stalemate
8. incidental
9. dynamic
10. inhibited

Lesson 62

1. e
2. d
3. c
4. b
5. a
6. remiss
7. harrowing
8. adamant
9. fatigued
10. supreme

Lesson 63

1. a
2. b
3. e
4. c
5. d
6. motivate
7. commence
8. bedlam
9. divert
10. welcome

Lesson 64

1. d
2. a
3. e
4. b
5. c
6. acclaim
7. aloof
8. magnetic
9. residual
10. audacious

Lesson 65

1. a
2. d
3. e
4. b
5. c
6. vim
7. thwart
8. novice
9. infused
10. colossal

Lesson 66

1. c
2. d
3. a
4. b
5. e
6. rectify
7. rue
8. versatile
9. quaint
10. instigated

Lesson 67

1. b
2. c
3. d
4. e
5. a
6. inspires
7. lunged
8. correlation
9. differentiate
10. laudable

Lesson 68

1. d
2. a
3. b
4. e
5. c
6. apparent
7. wealth
8. rancid
9. reveled
10. surly

Lesson 69

1. e
2. c
3. d
4. b
5. a
6. affable
7. atone
8. kindled
9. winced
10. thrive

Lesson 70

1. d
2. a
3. b
4. c
5. e
6. obligate
7. abbreviate
8. coach
9. wayward
10. gullible

Crossword Puzzle: Lessons 61-70

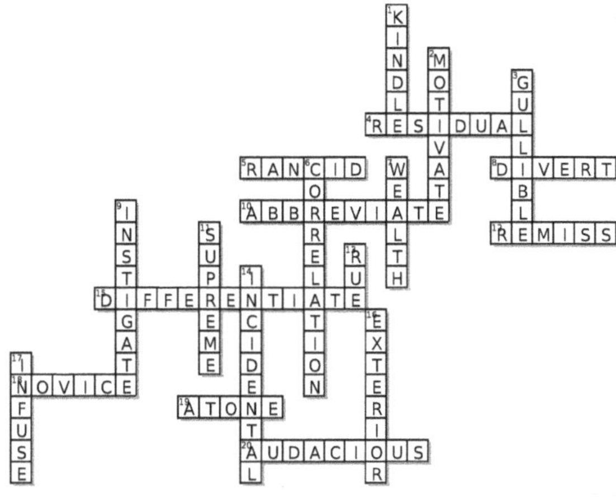

Review: Lessons 61-70

1. m
2. h
3. f
4. c
5. g
6. j
7. e
8. t
9. i
10. b
11. n
12. q
13. d
14. r
15. o
16. a
17. k
18. l
19. p
20. s

Lesson 71

1. a
2. b
3. d
4. e
5. c
6. ostracize
7. indicted
8. rankled
9. hovel
10. pragmatic

Lesson 72

1. e
2. b
3. c
4. a
5. d
6. depletes
7. thaw
8. absurd
9. polish
10. favor

Lesson 73

1. d
2. e
3. a
4. b
5. c
6. annihilated
7. bloated
8. discretion
9. swagger
10. retribution

Lesson 74

1. a
2. c
3. b
4. e
5. d
6. implored
7. unconditional
8. personable
9. illusion
10. grotto

Lesson 75

1. b
2. d
3. c
4. a
5. e
6. inevitable
7. astute
8. concise
9. desolate
10. abrogate

Lesson 76

1. e
2. a
3. b
4. d
5. c
6. forage

7. fortitude
8. accidental
9. imitate
10. indignation

Lesson 77

1. a
2. d
3. c
4. e
5. b
6. strategy
7. devout
8. prologue
9. frequent
10. sanction

Lesson 78

1. b
2. e
3. a
4. d
5. c
6. defunct
7. ostentatious
8. neutral
9. liberate
10. plentiful

Lesson 79

1. a
2. d
3. e
4. c
5. b
6. exorbitant
7. perceptive
8. acquire
9. squalid
10. elderly

Lesson 80

1. e
2. b
3. c
4. a
5. d
6. render
7. accentuate
8. belligerent
9. ponder
10. temperance

Word Search: Lessons 71-80

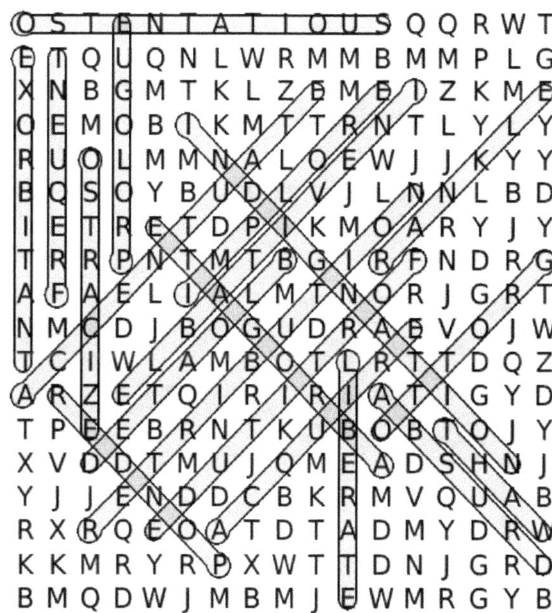

Review: Lessons 71-80

1. q
2. l
3. e
4. o
5. m
6. g
7. j
8. f
9. p
10. c
11. n

12. s
13. t
14. a
15. b
16. i
17. h
18. k
19. d
20. r

Lesson 81

1. d
2. c
3. b
4. e
5. a
6. monarch
7. desecrate
8. panorama
9. tortuous
10. heterogeneous

Lesson 82

1. c
2. a
3. b
4. e
5. d
6. contusion
7. comeback
8. amend
9. barrage
10. etiquette

Lesson 83

1. e
2. d
3. c
4. a
5. b
6. callous
7. nebula
8. enhance
9. surrogate
10. indicate

Lesson 84

1. e
2. c
3. d
4. a
5. b
6. dogmatic
7. specify
8. repetitive
9. redundant
10. boarders

Lesson 85

1. d
2. b
3. a
4. c
5. e
6. mitigate
7. inhabit
8. effect
9. inauspicious
10. founder

Lesson 86

1. b
2. c
3. d
4. a
5. e
6. tranquility
7. debonair
8. stanza
9. plead
10. lesion

Lesson 87

1. b
2. c
3. e
4. a
5. d
6. dissemble
7. prolific
8. innate
9. submerge
10. fallow

Lesson 88

1. e
2. b
3. d
4. a
5. c
6. epoch
7. kinetic
8. jubilee
9. valor
10. amiable

Lesson 89

1. b
2. c
3. d
4. e
5. a
6. schism
7. declamation
8. conciliate
9. ample
10. vanquished

Lesson 90

1. d
2. c
3. e
4. b
5. a
6. torpid
7. ecstatic
8. pathology
9. ethereal
10. obtuse

Crossword Puzzle: Lessons 81-90

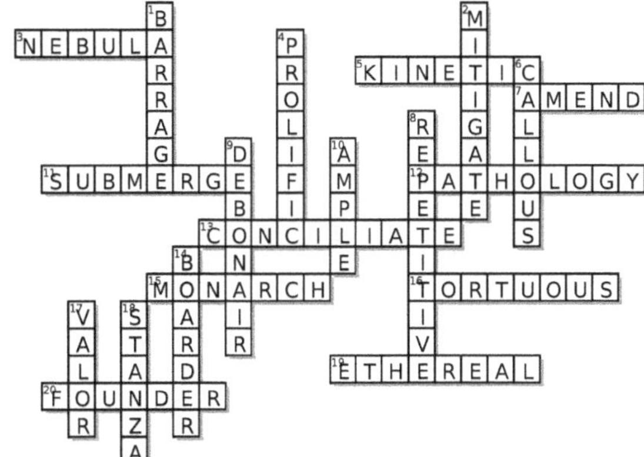

Review: Lessons 81-90

1. p
2. g
3. f
4. d
5. t
6. a
7. m
8. h
9. o
10. r
11. n
12. b
13. e
14. k
15. s
16. j
17. c
18. l
19. i
20. q

GLOSSARY

This glossary contains definitions of the new words from every lesson contained in this book. Please note that not every meaning of each word is contained in this glossary. Generally, only the most commonly used meanings of the words below are defined.

All entries in the glossary take the following form:

word (lesson): (part of speech) definition

Key for parts of speech:
adj. = adjective | n. = noun | v. = verb

abash (18): (v.) to cause to feel embarrassed, disconcerted, or ashamed

abbreviate (70): (v.) to shorten a word, phrase, or text

abrogate (75): (v.) to repeal or do away with a law, right, or formal agreement

absurd (72): (adj.) wildly ridiculous, insensible, or foolish

accentuate (80): (v.) to make more prominent or noticeable

accidental (76): (adj.) happening by chance, unintentionally, or unexpectedly

acclaim (64): (n.) enthusiastic public praise; (v.) to praise enthusiastically and publicly

accrue (3): (v.) (of sums of money or benefits) to be received by someone in regular or increasing amounts over time

accumulate (60): (v.) to gather together or acquire an increasing number or amount of

acquaintance (50): (n.) 1. a person's knowledge or experience of something; 2. a person one knows slightly but who is not a close friend

acquiesce (33): (v.) to accept something reluctantly and without protest

acquire (79): (v.) 1. to buy or obtain an object; 2. to learn or develop a specific skill or skill set; 3. to achieve a reputation as a result of one's behavior or activity

adamant (62): (adj.) refusing to be persuaded or change one's mind

additional (21): (adj.) added, extra, or supplementary to what is already given

adorn (51): (v.) to make more beautiful or attractive

adroit (17): (adj.) clever or skillful in using the hands or mind

adversity (51): (n.) difficulty or misfortune

affable (69): (adj.) friendly, easy to talk to, good-natured

aggrandize (41): (v.) to increase the power, status, or wealth of

aghast (16): (adj.) filled with shock or horror

ailment (55): (n.) an illness (typically minor illness)

akin (14): (adj.) of similar character

alleviate (53): (v.) to make pain or suffering less severe

aloof (64): (adj.) not friendly or forthcoming; cold; distant

alternate (10): (adj.) 1. every other; every second; 2. taking the place of; (n.) a person who acts as a substitute; (v.) to occur in turn repeatedly

amalgamation (53): (n.) the action, process, or result of uniting or combining

amass (38): (v.) to gather together or accumulate over a time period; to gather together in a group or crowd

ambulatory (12): (adj.) related to or adapted to walking

amend (82): (v.) to modify or make better, more accurate, or up-to-date by implementing small changes in something

amiable (88): (adj.) friendly and pleasant

amity (60): (n.) a friendly relationship

amorphous (39): (adj.) without a clearly defined shape or form; vaguely defined

ample (89): (adj.) enough or more than enough; large and plentiful; large and accommodating

annihilate (73): (v.) to destroy completely; to obliterate

annul (42): (v.) to declare an official agreement, decision, or result invalid

antidote (18): (n.) a medicine taken to counteract a particular poison

antisocial (8): (adj.) 1. not friendly; not wanting the company of others; 2. contrary to the laws and customs of society

apparent (68): (adj.) clearly visible or true, obvious; seemingly true

appliance (34): (n.) a device or piece of equipment designed to perform a specific task, typically a domestic one

approval (40): (n.) the action of officially agreeing on something or accepting something as satisfactory

arbitrator (17): (n.) an independent person or body officially appointed to settle a dispute

ardor (45): (n.) enthusiasm or passion

arid (43): (adj.) land and climate that is dry and barren that is hardly capable of supporting vegetation

arrogant (43): (adj.) having or revealing an exaggerated sense of oneself or one's abilities

articulate (7): (adj.) having the ability to speak fluently and coherently; (v.) to express an idea or feeling fluently and coherently

ascertain (26): (v.) to find something out for certain; to make sure of

astute (75): (adj.) having the ability to accurately assess situations or people and turn them to one's advantage

atone (69): (v.) to make amends or reparation

atrocity (34): (n.) an extremely wicked or cruel act, often involving physical violence or injury

audacious (64): (adj.) 1. showing a willingness to take bold risks; 2. showing an impudent lack of respect

authentic (49): (adj.) genuine, of undisputed origin; based on facts, accurate, reliable

authoritarian (55): (adj.) favoring or enforcing strict obedience to authority, especially the government at the expense of personal freedom; showing a lack of concern about the wishes or cares of others

B

bard (15): (n.) a poet, especially one conveying epics in an oral tradition

barrage (82): (n.) a concentrated outpouring or firing of something; (v.) to bombard someone with something

basis (48): (n.) the underlying support or foundation for an idea, argument, or process

bedlam (63): (n.) a scene of uproar and confusion

belligerent (80): (adj.) hostile and aggressive

beneficial (2): (adj.) favorable or advantageous; resulting in good

benevolent (44): (adj.) well-meaning and kindly

berate (44): (v.) to scold or criticize someone angrily

beverage (52): (n.) a drink

bland (12): (adj.) lacking strong features or characteristics and therefore uninteresting; food or drink that is mild and insipid; a person lacking strong emotion and unremarkable

blasphemy (36): (n.) the act of speaking sacrilegiously about God or things that are sacred

blend (7): (n.) a mixture of different things or qualities; (v.) to mix a substance with another so that they meld together as a mass; to put abstract things together; a harmonious combination

bloated (73): (adj.) 1. (of the body) swollen with fluid or gas; 2. excessive in size or amount

blueprint (48): (n.) a design plan or technical drawing (used heavily in architecture); something that acts as a plan, model, or template

boarder (84): (n.) a person (often a student residing at school) who receives regular meals when staying somewhere

brevity (19): (n.) concise and exact use of words in speech; shortness of time

brusque (22): (adj.) abrupt or offhand in speech or manner

buffer (27): (n.) a person or thing that prevents incompatible or antagonistic people or things from coming into contact with or harming each other; (v.) to lessen or moderate the impact of something

buffet (24): (n.) a meal consisting of several dishes in which guests serve themselves; (v.) to strike repeatedly; to batter; to knock someone over or off course

C

caliber (8): (n.) 1. the quality of someone's character or the level of someone's ability; 2. the internal diameter or bore of a gun barrel

callous (83): (adj.) exhibiting an insensitive and cruel disregard for others

candid (10): (adj.) truthful and straightforward; frank

cavity (38): (n.) an empty space within a solid object, especially the human body; the decayed part of a tooth

cavort (57): (v.) to jump or dance around excitedly

celestial (3): (adj.) of or pertaining to the sky or the heavens

choreography (33): (n.) the sequence of steps and movements in dance or figure skating

clash (37): (n.) 1. a violent confrontation; 2. a color mismatch; 3. a loud, jarring sound made by clashing metal objects together

cling (38): (v.) to hold on tightly to; to remain stubbornly persistent or faithful to something

clone (15): (n.) an identical copy of something; (v.) to make an identical copy of

coach (70): (1.) a horse-drawn or motor carriage; 2. a railway car; 3. an athletic instructor or trainer; (v.) to instruct or train athletes

collaborate (25): (v.) to work jointly on an activity, especially to produce something

colossal (65): (adj.) extremely large

comeback (82): (n.) 1. a return by a well-known person to the field in which they were originally successful; 2. a quick reply to a critical remark

commence (63): (v.) to begin, start

conciliate (89): (v.) to stop someone from being angry; to placate; to pacify

concise (75): (adj.) giving much information in few words

conduit (19): (n.) a channel for conveying a fluid; a person or organization that acts as a channel for the transmission of something

congenial (46): (adj.) 1. (of a person) pleasant because of a personality, interests, or other qualities similar to one's own; 2. (of a thing) pleasant or suitable because it is suited to one's tastes or inclination

conspicuous (15): (adj.) standing out so as to be clearly visible

constant (38): (n.) continuous and unchanging; remaining the same over a period of time; referring to a person who is faithful

contusion (82): (n.) a bruise

convene (7): (v.) to come or bring together for a meeting or activity; to assemble

convenient (29): (adj.) fitting in well with one's needs, activities, and/or plans

convey (20): (v.) to transport or carry from place to place; to make an idea, impression, or feeling known or understandable to someone

copious (28): (adj.) abundant in supply or quantity

correlation (67): (n.) a mutual relationship or connection between two or more things

covert (50): (adj.) not openly acknowledged or displayed

craft (42): (n.) an activity involving skill and often making things by hand; (v.) to exercise skill in making or doing something

credulous (45): (adj.) exhibiting too great a readiness to believe things

crisis (46): (n.) a period of intense difficulty, danger, or trouble

culpable (41): (adj.) worthy of blame

culture (43): (n.) the arts and other manifestations of human intellectual achievement regarded collectively

custom (58): (adj.) made or done for a particular customer; (n.) a traditional and widely accepted way of behaving or doing something that is specific to a particular society, place, or time

D

debonair (86): (adj.) (of a man) stylish, charming, and confident

declamation (89): (n.) a speech delivered in a rhetorical or passionate way

deficiency (11): (n.) a lack or shortage

defunct (78): (adj.) no longer existing or functioning

deliberate (9): (adj.) done consciously and intentionally; (v.) engage in long and careful consideration

deluge (55): (n.) a severe flood; (v.) to flood or be flooded by a great quantity of something

demonstrate (44): (v.) 1. to clearly show the existence or truth of something by giving proof or evidence; 2. to take part in a public meeting or protest expressing views on a political issue

deplete (72): (v.) to use up the supply or resources of

deplore (49): (v.) to feel or express strong disapproval of (something)

desecrate (81): (v.) to treat something sacred with disrespect

desolate (75): (adj.) deserted of people and in a state of bleak and dismal emptiness

despondent (39): (adj.) in low spirits from loss of hope or courage

detour (35): (n.) a long and roundabout route taken to avoid something or to visit somewhere along the way; (v.) to take a long or roundabout route

detrimental (21): (adj.) tending to cause harm

devout (77): (adj.) having or showing deep religious feeling or commitment

differentiate (67): (v.) to recognize or figure out what makes something different

diligent (1): (adj.) having or showing care and conscientiousness in one's work or duties

discreet (25): (adj.) careful and circumspect in one's speech or actions, especially in order to avoid causing offense or to gain an advantage

discretion (73): (n.) the quality of behaving in such a way that offence is not caused or private information is not revealed

disposition (3): (n.) 1. a person's inherent qualities of mind and character; 2. the way in which something is placed or arranged, especially in relation to other things

dissemble (87): (v.) to conceal one's true intentions, beliefs, or feelings

distress (41): (n.) 1. extreme anxiety, sorrow, or pain; 2. troubles caused by lacking money or basic life necessities; (v.) to cause somebody anxiety, sorrow, or pain

divert (63): (v.) 1. to cause someone or something to change course or turn from one direction to another; 2. to distract someone or his or her attention from something

dogged (47): (adj.) having or showing tenacity and grim persistence

dogmatic (84): (adj.) inclined to lay down principles as absolute truth

domicile (43): (n.) the country that a person treats as his or her permanent home

dose (29): (n.) a quantity of a medicine or drug (or something analogous and unpleasant) recommended to be taken at a particular time; (v.) to administer a quantity of a medicine or drug to someone

drone (20): (n.) a low, continuous humming sound; (v.) to make a continuous low humming sound; to speak tediously in a monotonous tone

dutiful (45): (adj.) conscientiously or obediently fulfilling one's role

dynamic (61): (adj.) characterized by constant change, activity, or progress

E

eccentric (52): (adj.) 1. unconventional and slightly strange; 2. off-center (n.) a person with unconventional and slightly strange behavior

ecstatic (90): (adj.) feeling overwhelming joy or excitement

effect (85): (n.) 1. a change that is the result of another action or cause; 2. the extent to which something succeeds or is operative; 3. an impression produced in the mind of a person; (v.) to cause something to happen or bring about

effectual (28): (adj.) (typically of something abstract or inanimate) successful in producing a desired or intended result; effective

egress (9): (n.) an exit

elderly (79): (adj.) a person who is old or showing signs of aging

election (54): (n.) a formal organized process of selecting or being selected, typically for members of a political party

embrace (1): (n.) the act of holding someone closely in one's arms; (v.) 1. to hold someone closely in one's arms; 2. to accept or support a belief, theory, or change willingly and enthusiastically; 3. to include or contain something as a constituent part

encounter (44): (n.) an unexpected or casual meeting with someone or something; (v.) 1. to unexpectedly experience or be faced with something difficult or hostile; 2. to meet

encumber (2): (v.) to restrict or burden someone or something in such a way that free action or movement is difficult; to saddle a person with debt or mortgage; to fill or block up (a place)

endeavor (6): (n.) an attempt to achieve a goal; an enterprise or undertaking; (v.) to try hard to do or achieve something

enhance (83): (v.) to intensify, increase, or improve the quality of something

enlighten (4): (v.) to give (someone or several people) greater knowledge and understanding about a subject or situation

enthrall (3): (v.) to capture the fascinated attention of

entity (29): (n.) a thing with a distinct, independent existence

epoch (88): (n.) a period of time in one's life or in a historical period marked by notable events; (geology) a long time period that is divided into ages

erratic (16): (adj.) uneven in pattern or movement

erroneous (4): (adj.) wrong, incorrect

ethereal (90): (adj.) 1. feeling too light or delicate for the world; 2. heavenly or spiritual

etiquette (82): (n.) the customary code of appropriate behavior in society; manners

euphoria (34): (n.) a feeling or state of intense happiness or excitement

evacuate (26): (v.) 1. to remove someone (or several people) from a place of danger to a safe place; 2. to remove air, water, or other contents from a container

exorbitant (79): (adj.) a price or amount charged that is unreasonably high

exquisite (59): (adj.) extremely beautiful and delicate; intensely felt; highly sensitive or discriminating

exterior (61): (adj.) forming, existing on, or related to the outside of something; (n.) the outer surface or structure of something

extol (26): (v.) to praise

extravagant (10): (adj.) lacking restraint in spending money or resources; exceeding what is reasonable or appropriate

F

facile (24): (adj.) easily achieved or effortless; superficial

fallow (87): (adj.) farmland that is ploughed and harrowed but left uncultivated to restore its fertility for crop production

famine (37): (n.) an extreme scarcity of food

fanatic (28): (n.) a person filled with excessive single-minded passion, often for an extreme religious or political cause

fatigue (62): (n.) extreme tiredness, especially resulting from mental or physical exertion or illness

favor (72): (n.) an attitude of approval or liking; 2. an act of kindness beyond what is due or necessary; (v.) to show approval or preference for

feat (53): (n.) an action or achievement that requires great courage or skill

ferocious (6): (adj.) savagely fierce, cruel, or violent

fiasco (29): (n.) a complete failure, usually in a ludicrous or humiliating way

fickle (1): (adj.) changing one's loyalties, interests, or affection frequently

fidelity (32): (n.) faithfulness to a person, cause, or belief as exhibited by continuing loyalty and support; faithfulness to a spouse

fissure (54): (n.) a long narrow opening made by cracking or splitting, especially in the earth; (v.) to split or crack something to cause a long narrow opening

flabbergast (37): (v.) to greatly surprise someone, to astonish

fling (37): (n.) a short period of enjoyment or wild behavior; (v.) to throw or hurl forcefully

fluctuate (48): (v.) to rise and fall irregularly in number or amount

flux (47): (n.) 1. the action or process of flowing or flowing out; 2. continuous change

focal (60): (adj.) of or relating to the center or main point of interest

forage (76): (v.) to search widely for food or provisions

forlorn (13): (adj.) pitifully sad, abandoned, or lonely

fortitude (76): (n.) courage in pain or adversity

founder (85): (n.) a person who establishes a business, organization, club, or institution; (v.) (usually of a ship) to fill with water and sink

frequent (77): (adj.) 1. occurring on many occasions, often, or habitual; 2. occurring in short distances apart; (v.) to visit a place often or habitually

fretful (40): (adj.) feeling or expressing distress or irritation

frivolous (25): (adj.) not having any serious purpose or value

frock (34): (n.) a woman's dress

G

gainsay (24): (v.) to deny or contradict a fact or statement

galactic (16): (adj.) of or relating to galaxies, especially the Milky Way

generalize (1): (v.) to make a general or broad statement by inferring from specific cases; to make something more widespread or common

gesture (53): (n.) a movement of the body, especially the hand or head, to express an idea or meaning, or to convey one's feelings or intentions; (v.) to move a part of the body, especially the hand or head, to express an idea or meaning, or to convey one's feelings or intentions

gloss (5): (n.) a shine or luster on a smooth surface; (v.) to conceal or disguise something by treating it briefly or representing it misleadingly

goodwill (24): (n.) friendly, helpful, or cooperative feelings or attitude

gourmand (32): (n.) one who enjoys eating and who often eats too much

grant (20): (n.) a sum of money given by an organization, especially a government, for a particular purpose; (v.) 1. to agree to give or allow (something requested) to; 2. to agree or admit to someone that something is true

graphic (9): (adj.) 1. of or related to visual art; 2. giving a vivid picture with explicit detail; (n.) a pictorial item displayed on a screen or stored as data

gregarious (56): (adj.) a person who is fond of company, sociable

grotto (74): (n.) a small picturesque cave, especially a fake one in a garden or park

grovel (33): (v.) to lie or move abjectly on the ground with one's face downward

gullible (70): (adj.) credulous; easily persuaded to believe something

H

harrowing (62): (adj.) acutely distressing

harsh (7): (adj.) unpleasantly jarring to the senses or rough; cruel or severe

hasten (4): (v.) to be quick to do something; to move hurriedly

heirloom (13): (n.) a valuable object that has belonged to a family for several generations

herculean (18): (adj.) requiring great strength or effort

heterogeneous (81): (adj.) diverse in content or in character

hovel (71): (n.) a small and squalid dwelling

humble (56): (n.) 1. having or showing a modest or low estimate of one's importance; 2. of low social, administrative, or political rank; (v.) to lower (someone) in dignity or importance

I

idiom (37): (n.) a group of words having an established meaning that is not deducible from the words themselves

ignoble (9): (adj.) not honorable in character or in purpose

illegible (35): (adj.) not clear enough to be read

illusion (74): (n.) a thing that is likely to be wrongly perceived by the senses; a deception; a false idea or belief

illustrate (21): (v.) 1. to provide (a book, newspaper, etc.) with pictures; 2. to explain or make something clear by way of charts, pictures, and other visuals; 3. to serve as an example of

imitate (76): (v.) to take or follow as a model; to copy someone else's mannerisms; to copy or simulate

imminent (9): (adj.) about to happen

implore (74): (v.) to beg someone earnestly to do something

impudent (21): (adj.) not showing due respect for another person

inauspicious (85): (adj.) unfavorable; unpromising

incidental (61): (adj.) accompanying but not a major part of something

incision (31): (n.) a surgical cut made into the skin or flesh

incite (57): (v.) to encourage or stir up (violent or unlawful behavior)

inclination (18): (n.) 1. a person's natural tendency to act in a particular way; a propensity or disposition; 2. a slope or slant; 3. the angle at which a straight line or plane intersects another

incoherent (22): (adj.) expressed in an incomprehensible or confusing way

incorrigible (33): (adj.) (of a person or his or her tendencies) unable to be corrected, reformed, or improved

incur (8): (v.) to become subject to (something unwelcome or unpleasant) as a result of one's own behavior or actions

indicate (83): (v.) 1. to point out or show; to briefly state something; to gesture; to show or register a reading (of a meter or gauge); 2. to suggest or show signs of a necessary course of action

indict (71): (v.) to formally accuse or charge with a serious crime

indignation (76): (n.) anger or annoyance caused by what is perceived as unfair treatment

inevitable (75): (adj.) certain to occur; unavoidable

infuse (65): (v.) to fill or pervade; to instill a quality in someone or something

ingenious (31): (adj.) clever, original, and inventive

inhabit (85): (v.) (of a person or animal) to live in a particular place or geographic region

inhibit (61): (v.) to hinder, restrain, or prevent an action or process; to make someone self-conscious and unable to act in a natural way

iniquity (19): (n.) immoral or grossly unfair behavior

initiate (50): (v.) 1. to cause something to begin; 2. to admit someone into a secret society or group

innate (87): (adj.) inborn or natural

innumerable (16): (adj.) too many to be counted (used often in exaggeration)

inspect (48): (v.) to examine someone or something closely to assess condition and/or shortcomings

inspire (67): (v.) to fill someone with the urge or ability to feel or do something

instantaneous (13): (adj.) occurring or done immediately

instigate (66): (v.) to bring about or initiate an action or event; to provoke

intellectual (1): (adj.) of or relating to use of mental faculties; possessing highly developed mental faculties; (n.) a person with highly developed mental faculties

intercept (42): (n.) an act or instance of obstructing someone or something so as to prevent it from continuing to a destination; (v.) to obstruct someone or something so as to prevent it from continuing to a destination

irrational (52): (adj.) not logical or reasonable

J

joyous (23): (adj.) full of happiness and excitement

jubilant (54): (adj.) feeling or expressing great happiness

jubilee (88): (n.) a special anniversary of an event (especially 25 years, 50 years, etc.)

juncture (14): (n.) a particular point in events or time; a place where things join

K

kiln (11): (n.) a furnace or oven for burning, baking, or drying, especially one for firing pottery

kindle (69): (v.) to light or set on fire; to arouse or inspire

kinetic (88): (adj.) of, concerning, or relating to motion

L

laceration (33): (n.) a deep cut in the skin or flesh

laudable (67): (adj.) praiseworthy; commendable

lesion (86): (n.) part of tissue or an organ that has suffered a cut, wound, ulcer, or abscess

levity (36): (n.) humor or frivolity; often treating a serious matter in a manner lacking due respect

lexicon (22): (n.) the vocabulary of a person, language, or branch of knowledge

liberate (78): (v.) to set someone free from a situation (esp. slavery or imprisonment); to free one from a situation that limits free thought or expression or has rigid social conventions; to free from enemy occupation

linchpin (4): (n.) a person or thing vital to an enterprise or organization

lithe (5): (adj.) (especially of a person's body) thin, supple, graceful

lore (17): (n.) a body of traditions and knowledge on a subject or held by a particular group, typically transmitted by word of mouth

lunge (67): (n.) a sudden forward thrust of the body typically to attack someone or to seize something; (v.) to make a sudden forward thrust with a part of the body or a weapon

magnetic (64): (adj.) 1. capable of being attracted by or acquiring the properties of a magnet; 2. very attractive or alluring

magnitude (59): (n.) 1. the size or extent of something; 2. size

malevolent (36): (adj.) having a desire to harm or do evil to others

mandatory (55): (adj.) required by law or rules; compulsory

manipulate (4): (v.) 1. to handle or control (a tool, mechanism, etc.) in a skillful manner; to edit, alter, or move text or data on a computer; 2. to control or influence a person or situation cleverly, unscrupulously, or unfairly; to alter data or present statistics so as to mislead

mar (10): (v.) to impair the appearance, to disfigure; to impair the quality of

margin (23): (n.) 1. the edge or border of something; 2. the amount by which a thing is won or falls short

marvel (51): (n.) an astonishing or wonderful person or thing; (v.) to be filled with wonder or astonishment

memento (35): (n.) an object kept as a reminder or souvenir of a person or event

mendicant (6): (adj.) given to begging; (n.) a beggar

menial (32): (adj.) (of work) not requiring much skill and of little prestige

merger (18): (n.) a combination of two things (usually companies) into one

migrate (35): (v.) to move from one region or habitat to another (often seasonally); to move from one country to another; to move from one part of something to another

miscellaneous (54): (adj.) (of items or people) of various types or from different sources

mitigate (85): (v.) to make less painful, serious, or severe

monarch (81): (n.) a sovereign head of state such as a king, queen, or emperor

mores (23): (n.) the fundamental customs and conventions of a community

motivate (63): (v.) 1. to provide someone with an objective for doing something; 2. to stimulate one's interest in doing something

mundane (59): (adj.) lacking excitement or interest; dull

muster (50): (v.) to summon up a feeling, attitude, or response

mute (51): (adj.) refraining from speech or temporarily speechless; (n.) a person without the power of speech; (v.) to deaden, muffle, or soften the sound of

N

nebula (83): (n.) 1. a cloud of gas in outer space; 2. any bright spot in the night sky

negative (28): (adj.) 1. consisting in or characterized by the absence rather than the presence of distinguishing features; 2. not desirable or optimistic; 3. characterizing a number less than zero

neutral (78): (adj.) 1. not helping or supporting either side in a conflict; 2. having no strongly marked positive or biased characteristics; 3. (physics) neither positively nor negatively charged; 4. (chemistry) neither acid nor alkaline

newfangled (25): (adj.) different from what one is used to; objectionably new

noisome (2): (adj.) having an extremely offensive smell; disagreeable; unpleasant

nomad (34): (n.) a person or a member of a people who travel from place to place

notice (12): (n.) 1. attention, observation; 2. notification or warning of something, especially to allow preparations to be made; 3. a displayed sheet giving news or information; (v.) to become aware of

novice (65): (n.) a person who is new or inexperienced in a field or situation

noxious (12): (adj.) harmful, poisonous, or very unpleasant

nucleus (46): (n.) the central and most important part of an object, group, or movement, forming a basis for its development and growth

O

oasis (27): (n.) a fertile spot in a desert where water is found

objectionable (26): (adj.) arousing distaste or opposition; unpleasant or offensive

obligate (70): (v.) to require, especially legally or morally

oblige (47): (v.) to make someone morally or legally bound to an action or course of action

obtuse (90): (adj.) 1. annoyingly insensitive or slow to understand; 2. an angle whose measure is greater than 90 degrees and less than 180 degrees

ominous (40): (adj.) giving the impression that something bad or unpleasant is about to happen

operate (25): (v.) 1. to control the functioning of a machine, process, or system; 2. to manage and run a business; 3. to perform a surgical procedure

opinion (23): (n.) a view or judgment formed about something, not necessarily based on fact or knowledge; a formal statement by an expert rendering advice or judgment on a matter

optimal (2): (adj.) best or most favorable

oration (21): (n.) a formal speech, ordinarily one that is given on a ceremonial occasion

ostentatious (78): (adj.) characterized by pretentious display meant to attract attention

ostracize (71): (v.) to exclude someone from a group or society

P

pacifist (49): (n.) one who believes war and violence are unjustifiable

paltry (22): (adj.) a small or meager amount of something; petty; trivial

panorama (81): (n.) 1. an unbroken view of a whole region surrounding an observer; 2. a complete survey or presentation of a sequence of events or a subject

pathetic (13): (adj.) arousing pity, especially through vulnerability or sadness; miserable; inadequate

pathology (90): (n.) the science of the causes and effects of disease

patron (23): (n.) 1. a person who gives financial support to another individual, a cause, an organization, or an activity; 2. a customer (typically a regular one)

perceptive (79): (adj.) exhibiting sensitive insight

personable (74): (adj.) (of a person) having a pleasant manner or appearance

physiognomy (60): (n.) a person's facial features or expression, especially when regarded as indicative of character or ethnic origin; the art of judging character from facial characteristics

pigment (19): (n.) the natural coloring of plant or animal tissue; a substance used for coloring or painting, especially a dry powder that, when mixed with water or oil, forms a paint or ink

plead (86): (v.) 1. to present an emotional appeal or to beg; 2. to present and argue for a particular position in a public context, especially a court

plentiful (78): (adj.) existing in great quantity; abundant

policy (39): (n.) a course or principle of action adopted or proposed by a government, party, business, or individual

polish (72): (n.) a substance that gives an object a smooth and shiny surface when the latter is rubbed; (v.) to make the surface of something smooth and shiny by rubbing it

pompous (31): (adj.) affectedly and irritatingly self-important or grand

ponder (80): (v.) to think carefully about something before making a decision

portly (40): (adj.) stout or fat (usually in reference to a man)

pose (13): (n.) 1. a way of standing or sitting, usually adopted in order to be photographed, drawn, or painted; 2. a particular way of behavior adopted in order to give others a false impression or to impress others; (v.) 1. to present or constitute (a problem, danger, or difficulty); 2. to assume a particular attitude in order to be photographed, drawn, or painted; 3. to behave affectedly in order to impress others

pragmatic (71): (adj.) practical; sensible; realistic

praise (5): (n.) the expression of approval or admiration of someone or something; (v.) to express warm approval of

predecessor (14): (n.) a person who held a job or office before another; a thing that has been followed or replaced by another

predicament (12): (n.) a difficult, unpleasant, or embarrassing situation

prevalent (40): (adj.) widespread over a particular area or at a particular time

prevaricate (20): (v.) to speak or act in an evasive way

prey (49): (n.) 1. an animal that is hunted or killed by another for food; 2. a person easily injured or taken advantage of; (v.) 1. to hunt and kill for food; 2. to take advantage of

priceless (20) : (adj.) so precious that its value cannot be determined

prior (39): (adj.) existing or occurring before in time, order, or importance

prolific (87): (adj.) 1. a plant animal or person producing much fruit, foliage, or offspring; 2. an author, artist, or composer who produces a great deal; 3. present in large numbers or quantities

prologue (77): (n.) an introductory section of a literary work or musical piece

prolong (48): (v.) to extend the duration of

prosperous (46): (adj.) flourishing financially; successful in material terms

protrude (39): (v.) to extend beyond or above a surface

pungent (47): (adj.) having a sharply strong smell or taste

pursuit (32): (n.) the act of following or chasing someone or something

Q

quaint (66): (adj.) attractively unusual or old-fashioned, often resembling small town or rustic life

quench (58): (v.) to satisfy one's thirst by drinking; to satisfy a desire

R

rancid (68): (adj.) (of foods) smelling or tasting unpleasant as a result of being old or stale

rankle (71): (v.) to cause persistent irritation, annoyance, or resentment

raze (8): (v.) to completely destroy (a building, town, or other site)

rebuff (36): (v.) to reject someone or something in an abrupt or ungracious manner

reception (11): (n.) 1. the action or process of receiving something sent, given, or inflicted; 2. a formal social occasion held to welcome someone or to celebrate a particular event; 3. the area in a hotel, office, or establishment where guests and visitors are greeted and dealt with

recognize (22): (v.) 1. to identify (someone or something) from having a previous encounter; 2. to acknowledge the existence, validity, or legality of

rectify (66): (v.) to set something right; to correct

redundant (84): (adj.) 1. superfluous; no longer needed to be useful or functioning; 2. words or data that can be omitted without loss of meaning

rejuvenate (56): (v.) to make someone or something feel fresher or younger

relish (8): (v.) to enjoy greatly

remiss (62): (adj.) lacking care or attention to duty; negligent

render (80): (v.) 1. to provide or give a service or help; 2. to cause to become or make; 3. to represent or depict artistically

rendezvous (35): (n.) a meeting at a specific time and place (typically between two people)

repetitive (84): (adj.) characterized by doing something over and over again or something happening over and over again often in a tiresome way

repress (15): (v.) to subdue someone or something by force; to restrain, prevent, or inhibit

repudiate (27): (v.) to refuse to accept or be associated with; to deny the truth or validity of

residual (64): (adj.) remaining after the greater part is gone; (n.) the remaining amount after other things have been subtracted or allowed for

restitution (42): (n.) 1. the act of returning something lost or stolen to its proper owner; 2. recompense for loss or injury; 3. the restoration of something to its original state

resuscitate (6): (v.) to revive someone from unconsciousness or apparent death; to make an idea or enterprise vigorous again

retort (43): (n.) a sharp, angry, or wittily incisive response to a remark; (v.) to respond to a remark or accusation in a witty or incisive manner

retract (17): (v.) to draw or be drawn back in; withdraw

retribution (73): (n.) punishment inflicted on someone as vengeance for a wrong or criminal act

revel (68): (v.) to enjoy oneself in a noisy and lively way; to delight in

rife (58): (adj.) (especially of something undesirable or harmful) of common occurrence; widespread

ruddy (3): (adj.) having a healthy red or reddish color; (v.) to make reddish in color

rue (66): (n.) repentance, regret, compassion, or pity; (v.) to bitterly regret

ruffle (38): (v.) to disturb the smoothness or tranquility of; to disorder or disarrange

rupture (30): (v.) (usually of a pipe, vessel, or bodily organ) to break or burst suddenly

S

sabbatical (52): (n.) a period of paid leave granted for study or travel

sanction (77): (n.) 1. a threatened penalty for disobeying a law or rule; 2. official approval or permission for an action; (v.) 1. to give official approval or permission for an action; 2. to impose a penalty on

sate (46): (v.) to fully satisfy a desire or appetite

scalpel (24): (n.) a surgical knife

scarce (5): (adj.) (of food, money, or another resource) insufficient for the demand; occurring in small numbers or quantities

schism (89): (n.) a split or division between strongly opposed parties or groups within a party caused by differences of opinion or belief

scour (31): (n.) the action of cleaning or brightening the surface of something by rubbing it hard, typically with an abrasive or a detergent; (v.) to clean or brighten the surface of something by rubbing it hard, typically with an abrasive or a detergent; 2. to subject a place or text to a thorough search in order to try to locate something

scourge (29): (n.) a person or thing that causes great trouble or suffering

sequential (60): (adj.) forming or following in a logical order

severe (49): (adj.) very great or intense; very strict or harsh

shirk (19): (v.) to avoid or neglect a duty or responsibility

shrewd (31): (adj.) having or showing sharp powers of judgment; astute

simulate (41): (v.) to imitate the appearance or character of

solid (26): (adj.) 1. firm and stable in shape, not liquid or fluid; 2. not hollow; 3. dependable, reliable; (n.) a substance that is firm and stable in shape and not a liquid or fluid

specify (84): (v.) to identify or state a fact clearly and definitely

splendid (27): (adj.) magnificent; very impressive

spontaneous (56): (adj.) performed by impulse and without any planning or premeditation

squalid (79): (adj.) 1. a place that is filthy and unpleasant, usually because of neglect or poverty; 2. exhibiting a lack of moral standards

stalemate (61): (n.) a situation where further action or progress by opposing parties seems impossible; a draw

stanza (86): (n.) a group of lines forming the basic metrical unit of a poem

strategy (77): (n.) a plan of action or policy designed with a specific aim

strenuous (47): (adj.) requiring or using great exertion

strive (30): (v.) to make great efforts to achieve or obtain something

submerge (87): (v.) 1. to place under water or some other liquid; 2. to completely cover or obscure

subsidy (36): (n.) a sum of money granted by the government or a public body to assist an industry or business so that the price of a commodity will remain affordable

succumb (42): (v.) to fail to resist (pressure, temptation, or some other force)

suffice (14): (v.) to be enough or adequate; to meet the needs of

summit (10): (n.) 1. the highest point of a hill or mountain; 2. a meeting between heads of government

supreme (62): (n.) superior to all others; strongest, most important, or most powerful; very great or intense

surly (68): (adj.) bad-tempered and unfriendly

surrogate (83): (n.) a substitute, especially another person deputizing for another in a specific role or office

suspend (59): (v.) 1. to temporarily prevent from continuing to be in force or in effect; to defer or delay an action or judgment; 2. to hang something from somewhere

swagger (73): (n.) a confident, arrogant, or aggressive walk; (v.) to walk in a confident, arrogant, or aggressive way

synopsis (54): (n.) a brief summary or general survey of something

T

tacit (14): (adj.) understood or implied without being stated

temperance (80): (adj.) moderation or self-restraint, especially from drinking

thaw (72): (v.) (usually of ice or snow) to become liquid or soft as a result of warming

theoretical (7): (adj.) concerned with or involving the abstract ideas of a field or study rather than its practical application

thrive (69): (v.) to flourish; to grow vigorously

thwart (65): (v.) to prevent someone from accomplishing something; to stymie

timid (58): (adj.) showing a lack of courage or confidence; frightened

timorous (57): (adj.) showing or suffering from nervousness, fear, or lack of confidence

torpid (90): (adj.) mentally or physically exhaustive; lethargic

tortuous (81): (adj.) twisting or winding

trade (41): (n.) 1. the action of buying and selling goods and services; 2. a job typically requiring manual skills and specialization; (v.) 1. to buy and sell goods and services; 2. to exchange something for something else, typically as a commercial transaction

tranquility (86): (adj.) calmness; serenity; peacefulness

transact (56): (v.) to conduct or carry out (business)

transparent (57): (adj.) 1. allowing light to pass through so that objects are easily seen; 2. easy to perceive or detect; having thoughts or feelings that are easy to detect

traumatic (28): (adj.) emotionally disturbing or distressing

trek (45): (n.) a long arduous journey, especially one made on foot

triumph (57): (v.) a great victory or achievement

tumult (17): (n.) a loud confused noise, especially one caused by a mass of people; confusion or disorder

unconditional (74): (adj.) not subject to any stipulations or limitations

underlying (55): (adj.) to be the cause or basis of

undermine (45): (v.) to damage or weaken something (often an intellectual argument)

unilateral (27): (adj.) 1. (of an action or decision) performed by or affecting only one person, group, or country involved in a particular situation, without the agreement of another or the others; 2. relating to, occurring on, or affecting only one side of an organ or structure, or of the body

universal (51): (adj.) of or done by all people

unruly (52): (adj.) disorderly, disruptive, and not amenable to discipline or control

usurp (32): (v.) to take a position of power or importance illegally or by force

V

vague (11): (adj.) of uncertain, indefinite, or unclear character or meaning

valor (88): (n.) courage in the face of danger

vanquish (89): (v.) to defeat thoroughly

variance (11): (n.) the fact or quality of being different, divergent, or inconsistent

verify (59): (v.) to ensure that something is true, accurate, or justified

versatile (66): (adj.) able to adapt to many different functions or activities

vex (58): (v.) to make one feel annoyed, frustrated, or worried, especially with trivial matters

vim (65): (n.) energy; enthusiasm

vogue (30): (adj.) popular; fashionable; (n.) the prevailing fashion or style at a particular time

voluminous (50): (adj.) occupying much space

vouch (16): (v.) to assert or confirm from one's experience that something is true or accurately as described

vulnerable (53): (adj.) susceptible to physical or emotional harm

wan (30): (adj.) (of skin) pale and weak, giving the impression of illness or exhaustion

warp (6): (v.) to bend or cause to become bent out of shape, typically because of dampness

warrant (30): (n.) a document issued by a legal or government official authorizing the police or some other body to make an arrest, search premises, or execute some other action to carry out justice; (v.) to justify or necessitate a course of action

wary (44): (adj.) feeling or showing caution about possible dangers or problems

wax (2): (v.) to become larger or stronger

wayward (70): (adj.) difficult to predict or control because of unusual or perverse behavior

wealth (68): (n.) an abundance of valuable possessions or money; plentiful supplies of a particular resource

weather (5): (n.) the state of the atmosphere at a place and time as regards heat, precipitation, humidity, etc.; (v.) 1. to wear away and change the texture of something by long exposure to the atmosphere; 2. to come safely through a storm or turbulent situation

welcome (63): (adj.) (of a guest or new arrival) gladly received; (n.) an instance or manner of greeting someone; (v.) 1. to greet someone arriving in a glad or friendly way; 2. to react with pleasure or approval to an event or development

wince (69): (n.) a slight grimace or recoiling caused by pain or distress; (v.) to grimace, shake, or recoil as the result of pain or distress

Y

yield (15): (n.) the full amount of an agricultural or industrial product; (v.) 1. to produce or provide; to generate; 2. to give way to arguments, demands, pressure, or traffic

www.ingramcontent.com/pod-product-compliance
Lightning Source LLC
LaVergne TN
LVHW061203120826
845149LV00011B/1892

* 9 7 8 0 9 9 8 4 8 4 1 7 4 *